What People Ar

M000042171

Deanna Harrison has written a powerful book about how to deal with the pain of forced termination from a church. She correctly observes that you never "get over" such an event. It is an experience that exposes all the elements of grief. Deanna skillfully weaves biblical principles, psychological findings, and staggering statistics to provide hope that God can bring healing and recovery to individuals and families who face the trauma of forced termination. If you've experienced this heartache, or know someone who has, this book is a valuable resource.
— Pastor David O. Dykes
  Green Acres Baptist Church, Tyler, Texas

Moving On by Deanna Harrison is an unusually insightful and practical book on forced termination while in ministry. It is chock full of solid theological and practical counsel for ministry families who are walking that difficult road. Through her own life story, Deanna offers others hope, healing and a balanced biblical perspective. I highly recommend!
— Susie Hawkins
  Author, speaker, minister's wife, Dallas, Texas

I have a unique appreciation for Deanna's story. As one directing mental health services to thousands of ministry families for over a decade, I saw firsthand the devastating impact of forced termination. As a son of a minister who followed his father's footsteps in ministry and experienced the joys and challenges of ministry before entering the mental health field, I have nothing but praise for *Moving On*. It is very well done, spiritually and psychologically.
– Dan McGee, Ph.D., author, teacher, counselor
    President, Dan McGee Associates, Inc.

This book is an essential read for all church folk, and serves as a lifesaving guide for those dealing with recovery from forced termination. Part devotional, part Bible Study, and part support group, Deanna's honest expression of her journey is well researched, well written, and well lived.
– Debbie Tudor, MS, LPCS
    Rockwall Counseling, PA

Moving On should be required reading for any layperson who serves in church leadership. Ministers, their spouses and families will find Deanna Harrison's book to be a healing journey. *Moving On* is a valuable contribution to a conversation that needs to start between the people who sit in the pews and those who stand in the pulpits all across America. Five Stars!
– Pastor James Shupp
    Author, *Who Killed My Church?*

To be "terminated" is far more than being fired or forced to resign. It is a death of identity, calling, relationship and love. For some reason, churches and ministries do it badly and it destroys people unless, like Deanna and her husband, they make the choice to live again.

– Fred Smith, President
The Gathering

The ministry families that are exposed to the un-Christlike behaviors associated with forced termination are negatively affected for years to come. Deanna Harrison shares her family's experience with forced termination in *Moving On*. Because it is often so difficult to heal from such an experience, I appreciate the work Deanna provides in this book on her process of healing. Those who have been subjected to this traumatic experience will find biblical and practical advice for moving on.

– Marcus N. Tanner, Ph.D., LMFTA
Texas Tech University & Founder of HealingChoice

MOVING ON

SURVIVING THE GRIEF OF FORCED TERMINATION

DEANNA HARRISON

aBM

Published by:
A Book's Mind
PO Box 272847
Fort Collins, CO 80527
www.abooksmind.com

Copyright © 2016 Deanna Harrison.
All Rights Reserved.
ISBN: 978-1-939828-54-5
Printed in the United States of America

No part of this document may be reproduced or transmitted in any form or by any means, electronic, mechanical, photocopying, recording, or otherwise, without prior written permission of the author. Unless otherwise noted, Scripture quotations are from the *New Living Translation*.

All names and some details have been altered for the protection and privacy of each individual and couple who have graciously shared their stories in the following pages.

For Marsha

Table of Contents

Acknowledgments I

Preface..III

Introduction VII

Psalm 43...IX

Part 1: The Elements of Grief

Chapter One—This Can't Be Happening: Denial and Disbelief...1

Chapter Two—Praying Down the Wrath of God: Anger...............9

Chapter Three—If Only: Bargaining...23

Chapter Four—Slogging Through the Fog: Depression 29

Chapter Five—Coming to Grips with Reality: Acceptance 35

Part 2: The Journey Continues

Chapter Six—Praying in Grief 51

Chapter Seven—Parenting in Grief...61

Chapter Eight—The Power of Response 69

Chapter Nine—Epilogue 81

Appendix

An Open Letter to Churches..89

Resources for Surviving the Grief of Forced Termination 99

About the Author 103

Acknowledgments

To all of the clergy couples who graciously shared their journeys of grief with me, thank you. This book would not have been complete without your wisdom and insight. Revisiting the events that shattered your lives was a painful task; I know that full well. May God grant each of you a special healing touch, and may He use this book to bring about healing to other couples who find themselves moving on.

Preface

Many years ago I wrote an article for a ministers' magazine on the topic of death. As a pastor's daughter and a pastor's wife, I knew firsthand the difficulty of ministering to people who were grieving. My research for the article included studying the five stages of grief first proposed by Elisabeth Kübler-Ross in her book *On Death and Dying*. Initially, professionals applied the theory of the grief process to physical death. Eventually, however, people began to see that the stages applied to more than physical death. People who face other traumatic events experience the same stages when the event leads to the death of their dreams. I never imagined back then I would one day find myself immersed in the grief process, not because a loved one died but because our ministry died.

But when our ministry at a church we deeply loved came to an abrupt halt, it didn't take long to realize I had plunged into the depths of grief. Our dreams for our ministry, our family and our retirement died overnight, leaving our lives shattered. Over the course of the next five years, I would work my way through grief as I tried to move on with life. At some point I came to realize that, in my experience, grief consists of elements rather than stages. It's a matter of semantics, I suppose, but the idea of "stages" of grief implies we eventually master a stage and move to the next and the next until ultimately we recover. But recovery is not the goal. The goal is to move on and live victoriously, with grief as part of life. So allow me, if you will, to refer to "elements" of grief rather than "stages."

The goal is to move on and live victoriously, with grief as part of life.

Though some people may progress through the elements of grief in a linear fashion, I did not. My journey amounted to a muddled mess. Two steps forward, one step back. One step forward. Bog down. At times I felt like I was slogging through molasses. But the goal remained the same: moving on.

Determining how to organize all of my thoughts for this book presented a major challenge. Ultimately, I chose to use the elements of grief as the framework around which I share my story. But even then, I've struggled to figure out where particular details should belong since many could go in multiple sections. Quite frankly, the anger and depression elements of my journey so tightly intertwined that dividing the content into separate chapters proved problematic. Like I said, my life had dissolved into a muddled mess.

If you find yourself immersed in the grief process because circumstances beyond your control have damaged or destroyed your ministry, I grieve with you. I pray that *Moving On* will help ease your pain as you make your journey of grief. Regardless of where you find yourself today, remember that you are in a process and the process takes time. If you're not familiar with the elements of grief, let me share a few thoughts concerning the journey:

♦ Even though you typically find the elements listed in the order of denial, anger, bargaining, depression and acceptance, you will not necessarily experience them in that order. If you're like me, you'll skip around or you'll experience multiple elements simultaneously. Or you might not experience every element. That's fine. Each journey is profoundly personal, which explains why each journey is extremely lonely.

♦ You will spend different amounts of time in different elements. Again, that's fine. You cannot rush the grieving process. Taking care of yourself as you move in and among the elements must become your top priority. Recognize that numerous factors influence every facet of your journey. Your own physical, mental, emotional and spiritual makeup *before* you began this journey of grief will impact your experience as you try to heal.

♦ There is no one correct way to travel the journey of grief. Each of us has his or her own deeply personal journey and no one can make it for us. Our journeys may resemble each other, and you may find yourself saying, "I felt that same way," but no two journeys evolve identically. Allow yourself the freedom to travel your journey however it unfolds. And if you're married, give your spouse that same freedom.

♦ Identify your feelings honestly. Christians often have a hard time admitting what's in their heart because they believe a "good Christian" wouldn't feel a particular emotion. Nonsense. Telling yourself you feel hurt when in reality a huge clump of hatred festers in your heart is like pretending you have a slight sore throat when in reality you've got strep. You'll never get the right medicine until you admit how you feel. And if you don't get the right medicine for strep, the infection can cause far more damage than just a sore throat. So face your feelings honestly or you'll delay the healing. God can't help you deal with what you're feeling until you admit it's there.

♦ Don't beat yourself up if you find yourself back in an element of grief you thought you'd resolved. Please treat yourself gently. You have experienced a traumatic event that has impacted every fiber of your being. Not one area of your life has escaped the effects of getting thrown out like yesterday's garbage. So wrap yourself in blankets of patience and gentleness as you travel your journey of grief.

Please do not mistake *Moving On* for a how-to book on getting over a forced resignation. In fact, you will never "get over" what has happened to you any more than someone "gets over" the death of a child or the diagnosis of a debilitating disease. Life will never be the same. *You* will never be the same. A loss as devastating as forced termination will either destroy us or transform us but we will not move on unchanged. The task awaiting each of us whose life has been shattered by forced termination is learning a new way to live. We must learn how to move on with life, even while learning to live with sorrow and grief.

The fact that I traveled my journey of grief and eventually arrived at the point of writing this book is due to a small handful of people: my husband, who traveled his own journey of grief and allowed me to travel mine, all the while reaffirming

The task awaiting each of us whose life has been shattered by forced termination is learning a new way to live.

his love for me and his commitment to our marriage; my parents and sisters, who prayed without ceasing; my father-in-law, who allowed us to put all of our worldly goods into storage and live with him; our children, who loved us and cried with us and offered sound advice; my sister-in-law, who always knew the right words to say; my one lifelong friend, the only non-family member who has stood by me throughout this journey; and the dear clergy couples who, upon the promise of anonymity, graciously shared their grief journeys with me as I researched this book. You will forever hold a special place in my heart.

Introduction

I was a pastor's wife for over 30 years. No one has ever been more suited to this role than I. I loved teaching Bible classes, singing in the choir, playing the organ, ringing handbells, leading retreats and hearing my husband preach Sunday after Sunday. I even enjoyed making hospital visits. I was, indeed, the ideal pastor's wife.

And then I wasn't.

For reasons beyond comprehension, our 30+ years of pastoral ministry came to an abrupt halt. I was still married to the same godly man of integrity but he was no longer a pastor. I was no longer a pastor's wife. Within days of learning anything was wrong, it was all over. We had been terminated. Our lives shattered as we plunged into a grief so deep I wondered if we would survive.

Perhaps you find yourself experiencing a similar grief. The years you invested in your ministry no longer matter to those you loved deeply and served faithfully. If so, then this book is for you. It's about a journey, my journey, to move through intense grief to discover life on the other side. I won't spend a lot of time sharing the details that caused our grief because the details don't really matter. If events beyond your control have derailed your ministry, then you know what really matters is learning to cope with shock, betrayal, anger, pain and overwhelming loneliness. You may wonder how you're going to survive emotionally, spiritually, financially, and even physically. Quite frankly, you may find yourself questioning how a loving God could have allowed such a thing to happen. I certainly did.

As I've traveled my journey of grief, I've discovered many, many ministry families who have had their lives and ministries shattered. We are legion. In fact, research indicates that between 23% and 41% of pastors either have or will experience at least one forced termination during their ministry.[1] And if they haven't experienced termination themselves, 91% of them know someone who has.[2]

If pastors haven't experienced termination themselves, 91% of them know someone who has.

Some of you have been forced out of your church because a new senior pastor arrived on the scene and wanted to bring in his own staff. Others of you were asked to resign because the church was declining and key leaders felt a new, younger pastor was needed to turn things around. Still others of you were terminated because you believed the church should go one direction and the lay leaders believed it should go another. Maybe you took a doctrinal or social position with which the deacons or elders disagreed. Or maybe a powerful church leader simply didn't like you. One former pastor is now selling cars because the wealthiest man in his church didn't like him. After several years of trying to run off the pastor, the man went to the deacons and offered to pay off the church's debt if they would fire the preacher.

They took the money.

When a minister's actions are immoral, illegal or unethical the church has no option but to take serious action, and termination may have to be a part of that action. But many, many times forced termination is undeserved. Being fired because the deacons want to get the church out of debt is clearly undeserved termination. At the very least, when termination is due to something other than an immoral or illegal issue the minister deserves time to find another place to serve rather than being tossed to the curb.

If you find yourself in this rapidly growing club of terminated clergy couples—a club for which you never desired membership—I pray that this book gives you a glimmer of hope you will survive. The journey ahead will be one of agonizing pain. There's simply no way to avoid the grief. But when you read the final page, I pray you will say, "She was able to move on. I will be able to as well."

1. Marcus N. Tanner, Jeffrey N. Wherry and Anisa M. Zvonkovic, "Clergy Who Experience Trauma as a Result of Forced Termination." *Journal of Religion & Health*, published online January 2012.
2. Ibid.

Psalm 43
(The Message)

Clear my name, God; stick up for me
against these loveless, immoral people.
Get me out of here, away
from these lying degenerates.
I counted on you, God.
Why did you walk out on me?
Why am I pacing the floor, wringing my hands
over these outrageous people?
Give me your lantern and compass,
give me a map,
So I can find my way to the sacred mountain,
to the place of your presence,
To enter the place of worship,
meet my exuberant God,
Sing my thanks with a harp,
magnificent God, my God.
Why are you down in the dumps, dear soul?
Why are you crying the blues?
Fix my eyes on God—
soon I'll be praising again.
He puts a smile on my face.
He's my God.

PART ONE

THE ELEMENTS OF GRIEF

This Can't Be Happening
Denial and Disbelief

Praying Down the Wrath of God
Anger

If Only
Bargaining

Slogging Through the Fog
Depression

Coming to Grips with Reality
Acceptance

This Can't Be Happening
Denial and Disbelief

You can never prepare yourself to lose a loved one. Whether the loved one dies after a long illness or in a sudden accident, nothing can prepare you for what follows.

The same thing is true for ministers. Whether your exit loomed for months or happened suddenly; whether you saw it coming or were blindsided; whether you were "fired," "terminated," "forced to resign" or "encouraged to take early retirement;" absolutely nothing can prepare you for the grief that follows.

> **When you lose an entire church family, the element of denial and disbelief creates the loneliest place in the world.**

We call the first element of grief denial. It encompasses those first few moments, minutes or days when your mind cannot wrap around your loss. During denial, your mind and body go on autopilot while waiting for your support system to assemble. You make the necessary phone calls. Church members activate prayer chains. Friends and family arrive.

That's how it works when you lose a loved one. But when you lose an entire church family, the element of denial and disbelief creates the loneliest place in the world.

In my case, denial lasted a matter of days before moving into disbelief. If you've known for months the end of your ministry was coming, you may have visited the element of denial a bit longer. You had more time to pray and beg God to intervene. You had time to play out various scenarios in your mind, all the while believing the worst would never happen. Not to you. Not to your spouse.

But sooner or later, reality sets in and denial turns to numbing shock and disbelief.

For weeks following our exit, I lived in shock and simply went through the motions of living. At night I'd crawl into bed, scoot up behind my husband and wrap my arms around him tightly, like two spoons in a drawer. If I dozed off, I'd awaken only to clear away the mental haze and realize all over again that I hadn't been dreaming. The nightmare was real and the pain was unbearable. Our ministry was over. It had died a sudden death and there was nothing I could do but get through another day. And getting through another day was hard work.

I'd wake up, shower, fix my hair and makeup, get dressed and drive to work. By that point in my grief journey, I'd lost so much weight I had to wear suspenders under heavy sweaters to hold up my slacks. When I looked in the mirror, a gaunt face with dull, lifeless eyes stared back at me. I had aged years within a matter of weeks. One day, a co-worker who didn't know about my husband's forced resignation saw me gazing into space. "What's wrong with you?" she asked. "You look like you're in pain."

Oh, if she only knew. In any other situation of grief, friends would have called to offer encouragement and support. They would have taken me to lunch and listened to my ramblings as I tried to sort out my thoughts. They would have written me notes and sent me beautiful greeting cards to lift my spirits. But none of those things ever happened. Oh, the first week after our termination we received a small handful of cards, but over the long months that followed, the mailbox remained empty. The phone remained quiet. One of the saddest moments of my journey came with the realization that many people had called themselves our "friends" simply because my husband held the title of pastor. I guess I'd always suspected that, but when our ministry was blown apart and only one woman occasionally called to say hello, the suspicion became a harsh reality.

It doesn't take an expert to know that when you're grieving, you need your friends to help you through the experience. But when your friends are church members and the whole reason you're grieving is because of what happened at the church . . . well, let's just say immense loneliness and intense grief became my intimate companions.

One minister's wife describes denial as "the heart stabbing pain of disbelief that played over in my mind again and again. In bed all hours of the night, and all day at work, so many thoughts rolled through my mind. I couldn't hold back the tears. My husband did not deserve this. Maybe someone would see the truth of the situation and straighten things out."

> "My husband did not deserve this. Maybe someone would see the truth of the situation and straighten things out." -Rebecca

But the whole truth rarely comes out, and if it does it's usually too late. The damage has been done, reputations have been destroyed and couples are left to face an uncertain and lonely future.

For months after our resignation, I continued my one-hour drive to and from work. I had always enjoyed the two hours of solitude. Those hours had provided time to think about life and the decisions laying before me at church and at work. But now the two hours alone with my thoughts proved unbearable. On most days, I'd make it to work without succumbing to my emotions. Maybe it was the fresh hope that my husband would receive positive news about a new job. Maybe it was the hope that someone would reach out to me and express compassion and concern. But those calls never came and at the end of the day, with hopes unfulfilled once again, I would sob on my drive home. Gut-wrenching, gasping-for-air sobs as I drove through heavy rush-hour traffic.

As I look back now, I'm convinced God sent angels to surround my car on those days when I couldn't see the road through my tears. He also gave me a prayer. During the time of grief's searing intensity, as I concentrated on putting one foot in front of the other and struggled to make sense of a senseless situation, Third Day released a song called "Revelation." The lyrics became the prayer that carried me through my long journey of grief:

My life,
Has led me down the road that's so uncertain
And now I am left alone and I am broken,
Trying to find my way,
Trying to find the faith that's gone
This time,
I know that You are holding all the answers
I'm tired of losing hope and taking chances,
On roads that never seem,
To be the ones that bring me home

Give me a revelation,
Show me what to do
'Cause I've been trying to find my way,
I haven't got a clue
Tell me should I stay here,
Or do I need to move
Give me a revelation
I've got nothing without You
I've got nothing without You

My life,
Has led me down this path that's ever winding
Through every twist and turn I'm always finding,
That I am lost again (I am lost again)
Tell me when this road will ever end

Give me a revelation,
Show me what to do
'Cause I've been trying to find my way,
I haven't got a clue

Tell me should I stay here,
Or do I need to move
Give me a revelation
I've got nothing without You
I've got nothing without...

I don't know where I can turn
Tell me when will I learn
Won't You show me where I need to go
Oh oh
Let me follow Your lead,
I know that it's the only way that I can get back home

Give me a revelation,
Show me what to do
'Cause I've been trying to find my way,
I haven't got a clue
Tell me should I stay here,
Or do I need to move
Give me a revelation
I've got nothing without You
I've got nothing without You

Oh, give me a revelation...

I've got nothing without You
I've got nothing without You

Copyright © 2008 Consuming Fire Music (ASCAP)
(adm. at CapitalCMGPublishing.com)
All rights reserved. Used by permission.

One day while driving home from work, "Revelation" came on the radio. Without thinking, I cranked up the volume and screamed over the music, "Can you hear this, God? This is me!" My head knew God would never leave me or forsake me, yet the intensity of my grief caused me to feel abandoned, not only by people but by God as well. I needed for God to hear my cry. I needed Him to look down from His throne in heaven and take notice of me—the emotionally distraught woman driving the little red SUV in the middle of heavy rush hour traffic—the woman who couldn't form a prayer but used "Revelation" as the cry of her heart. I desperately needed God to hear me. So, ridiculous as it seems now, I turned up the volume every time I heard "Revelation," just to ensure that God heard my cry.

Devotional Thought

Denial. Disbelief. Surely Joseph, son of Jacob, experienced these same emotions at various times in his life. During his early years he enjoyed the pleasures that came his way as Jacob's favorite son. But eventually the parental partiality caused his brothers to hate him. Genesis 37:4 says "when his brothers saw that their father loved him more than any of them, they hated him and could not speak a kind word to him."

The brothers' hatred plays out in verses 18-28 where we learn they would have killed Joseph had the oldest brother, Reuben, not stepped in and revised their plan. Instead of killing their kid brother, they ultimately sold him to a caravan of Midianite merchants for 20 pieces of silver. Within a matter of hours, Joseph's calling card changed from Father's Favorite to Subordinate Slave.

Surely in those first hours with the Midianites, Joseph must have felt the same anguish as clergy couples feel in the first element of grief.

> *Why did they betray me? They are my own brothers — I love them! What did I ever do to make them hate me with such intense hatred? If I did anything wrong, why didn't they give me a chance to make things right? Dear God, I feel so alone—I can't believe this is happening to me!*

The Scriptures do not tell us what went through Joseph's mind and heart until the climax of his story in Genesis 45 – 50. But there's no doubt his brothers' heartless actions deeply wounded him. Even though Genesis 39:2 tells us "the Lord was with Joseph and he prospered," God's presence did not remove the pain of his brothers' hatred and betrayal. Joseph would eventually refer to Egypt as "this land of my grief" (Gen. 41:52).

Any ministry couple forced to resign their church enters the land of grief, a sign flashing Denial and Disbelief marking the entrance into the land. You never dreamed you'd enter a land of such intense pain but here you are in your own personal hell. How will you survive this land? Only the Lord knows and it's His job to get you through. Your job is to keep putting one foot in front of the other. As Winston Churchill said to the British when they faced Nazi Germany, "If you're going through hell, keep going."

Father God, my heart and mind simply cannot comprehend the circumstances that have brought about such destruction in my life. I don't know how I will survive this land of grief. Hold on to me, Father, for I have no strength to hold on to You.

Praying Down the Wrath of God
Anger

When denial dissolves into disbelief, anger can't be far behind. In fact, anger flew in the door and took up residence right smack dab in the middle of my disbelief. I entered into a battle with anger that would last for several years. Our lives had been so completely shattered, our ministry so completely destroyed, we faced the daunting task of reinventing ourselves. Countless questions demanded answers. *Where would we live? What would we do? Who would we be?* We'd always been a pastor and pastor's wife. *Who would we be now?* The overwhelming task of starting an entirely new life was terrifying and yet we had no option. The decision had been made for us without our input on the matter. It's no wonder anger surfaced and resurfaced throughout the reinvention process. The moment I would think I'd dealt with all of the anger, it would rear its ugly head, sneering and hissing, reminding me the battle was not yet over.

Our lives had been so completely shattered, our ministry so completely destroyed, we faced the daunting task of reinventing ourselves.

Many Christians have a hard time dealing with anger. It is, perhaps, the easiest element of grief to suppress because we're not completely honest. We describe ourselves as feeling hurt, upset, aggravated or offended when the fact is, we're angry. Goodness knows I was angry. Full-blown, praying-down-the-wrath-of-God-on-my-enemies angry. And on top of that, I was angry with God. From my perspective, He had allowed evil to win and I couldn't understand why. In the midst of my grief I cried out to God. "Where are you? Why did you let this happen? Why didn't you intervene? You're the God of miracles, so why didn't you give one to us? What are we supposed to do? *Come on, God! Say something!*"

Anger clinched my soul and burned against church members, their words, and the irreversible damage that had destroyed our ministry. My husband experienced such intense grief I feared his heart would simply stop. During the first few weeks after our resignation, I invented reasons to call him from work. I'd ask about bringing home something for supper or tell him about a story I'd heard on the news, but my real reason for calling was my need to hear his voice—to know for certain at that moment his heart was still beating, even though it was so broken.

The anger I felt because of what happened to my husband is not unique to me. Other clergy couples admit they've fought their own battles with anger. And for many, they carry a sense of guilt for the anger they feel. Christians aren't supposed to get angry, we tell ourselves. Jesus came to give us an abundant life, not an angry life. So we mask our feelings with inaccurate labels and feel guilty on those occasions when we're honest enough to acknowledge what's really in our heart.

What is a Christian supposed to do with anger? After all, the Bible has a lot to say about the subject. The psalmist wrote that we should "refrain from anger" (Ps. 37:8 NIV). Solomon declared that "fools vent their anger" (Prov. 29:11) while "sensible people control their temper" (Prov. 19:11). In the New Testament, Jesus said "if you are even angry with someone, you are subject to judgment" (Matt. 5:22). James wrote that believers should be "slow to get angry" and then declared that "human anger does not produce the righteousness God desires" (Jas. 1:19-20). In Ephesians 4:31, Paul wrote, "Get rid of all bitterness, rage, anger, harsh words, and slander, as well as all types of evil behavior." In writing to the church at Colossae, he commanded the believers to put away a whole host of sins and anger topped the list (Col. 3:8). Galatians 5:22 lists the fruit of the Spirit and anger is nowhere to be found. Instead, anger ranks in the previous verses as something we should avoid, right along with sexual immorality, idolatry and sorcery (Gal. 5:18-20).

The only verse that offers any hope for Christians dealing with anger resides in Ephesians 4:26-27. Here Paul indicates it is possible to be angry without sinning. But, with all due respect, the passage doesn't tell us how to do that.

It's no wonder we have a difficult time successfully navigating the element of anger in our journey of grief. While there's no one right way to manage anger, I want to offer three suggestions to help you through the process.

Acknowledge your anger. Be honest with yourself. Admit you're angry. And by all means, admit to God you're angry. Not telling Him won't keep Him from knowing. And until you admit to God you're angry, you'll never ask Him to help you overcome your anger.

The intensity of your anger may surprise you. It certainly surprised me. I'd never felt anything so violent come out of my soul. Experts tell us that when a loved one dies, the degree of anger felt by the surviving spouse may reflect the degree of their love.[1] I think the same thing applies to those of us in ministry who grieve over the loss of a church family. If you served a church for many years, and if you deeply loved the members of your congregation, don't be surprised at the intensity of your anger.

Sam and Doris had served their congregation for nearly 25 years when church leaders forced them to resign. The issue? "My husband was friends with a businessman in the community and had been witnessing to him for several years. When the man announced that he was gay and was marrying his partner, the church demanded that my husband distance himself from him," Doris explained. When Sam refused to shun his friend, the church leaders demanded his resignation.

"Anger was burning inside of me," Doris told me. "How could they hurt my husband this way, a man who had served God so faithfully and loved and served the church?"

Not only did Doris feel angry, she felt helpless. "I saw my husband in such mental and spiritual anguish, and it broke my heart. He looked so pale and so sad and there was nothing I could say or do to help him."

This sense of helplessness provides a powerful fuel for the fires of anger. We're used to applying ointment and bandages to our children's wounds. We give hugs and kisses to make things better when our children hit rough patches in life. We prepare favorite foods and administer required medicines to bring about healing. And now, when people wound the person we love more than life itself, we're helpless to make the pain go away. "Only the Great Healer would be able to help him," one minister's wife said of her husband's pain.

But from my perspective, the Great Healer seemed to be taking an awfully long time. Month after month, one disappointment after another, the pain remained. And so did my anger. I repeatedly cried out during my journey of grief, "Dear God, I don't know what to do with the anger!"

God didn't miraculously remove the anger—that required a long process—but acknowledging its presence somehow removed some of its power. Telling God about my anger enabled me to say, "Yes, Anger, I know you're here. But you're not going to stay forever. I see you, God sees you, and together we're eventually going to get rid of you."

Determine to forgive. Anger and an unforgiving spirit live intertwined. An unforgiving spirit nourishes anger and helps it thrive. Forgiving people for the hurt they caused you is a critical step in the journey of grief.

As much as I wanted to turn back time and do something to prevent the horror that had become our life, I had to accept the fact there was nothing I could do to change what had happened. What was done was done. I could not close people's mouths. I could not open their eyes to see the truth. Minds were made up. Truth was irrelevant. There was nothing I could do to change the event that had shattered our lives.

Though I remained powerless to change what had happened, I did have the power to determine how I would respond. Clearly, I stood at a crisis point in my life. The experience was so brutal it would either crush me or it would change me in positive ways, though at the time I could not imagine anything good coming out of such intense suffering.

The experience was so brutal it would either crush me or it would change me in positive ways.

In the immediate weeks following our exit from the church we loved, one thought kept coming to mind: *You have to forgive them.* Did I want to forgive them? Never! And heaven knows I did not feel like forgiving. But I knew God required me to forgive. In the model prayer, Jesus taught His disciples to pray, "Forgive us our sins, as we forgive those who sin against us" (Luke 11:4). Later He would tell them, "But when you are praying, first forgive anyone you are holding a grudge against, so that your Father in heaven will forgive your sins, too" (Mark 11:25-26).

How could I ask God to forgive me for my sins if I didn't forgive those who had hurt me? Yet how could I ever forgive those people in the church who had destroyed our ministry and shattered our lives? And how could I forgive those who had remained on the sidelines, silently watching? How could I forgive them for not having the courage to stand up and shout, "No! This is wrong!"

I didn't want to forgive them, but I knew I had to. If I wanted to obey God, I had to choose to forgive. Forgiveness is a choice, but it is more than just saying, "I'm going to forgive and forget about it." For one thing, you will never forget the events that ended your ministry. You may never forget the words spoken or the sound of certain voices. Nothing will ever excuse what took place. But through the process of forgiveness, you will eventually arrive at the point where the memories do not bring intense, unbearable pain. The scars may always remain tender, but the pain will fade. It may take awhile—it took me five years—but the day will eventually come.

Don't expect to survive the element of anger on your own. That's like breaking your leg and saying, "I'm physically fit. My leg will heal just fine all by itself." No, it won't. And if you let it heal without expert attention, it will become infected and deformed. To avoid spiritual infection and deformity, you need to find resources to help guide you through the element of anger. Regardless of how strong your faith may be, you need all the support you can find to help you deal with anger in a healthy way.

A few resources to consider:

Anger by Gary Chapman

Letting Go of Anger: How to Get Your Emotions Under Control by Annie Chapman

Free Yourself to Love: The Liberating Power of Forgiveness by Jackie Kendall

Forgive and Forget: Healing the Hurts We Don't Deserve by Lewis B. Smedes

---

Anger is an element of grief we must move through, and for our sake and the sake of our family we need to move through it well. That doesn't mean we will conquer anger once and for all.

Anger passing in and out of our lives constitutes a natural part of living. Anger passing in and out of life presents a problem that requires attention. Allowing anger to take root, however, presents a major problem that will wreak havoc if left untended. When anger takes root, it causes numerous health issues. Medical research links prolonged anger to a host of problems including high blood pressure, high cholesterol, blocked arteries and heart disease. So it's important we learn to deal with anger as it arises. Our spiritual and physical health depend on it.

The Bible does not offer one specific passage of Scripture that outlines how to deal with anger, but many Scriptures support what today's experts recommend. Or put another way, today's experts advocate what the Bible has said all along:

First, relax—When we're angry our bodies produce stress hormones such as adrenaline and our breathing intensifies. Our blood pressure rises because our blood vessels constrict. That's why relaxation is one of the most important things you can do when you're angry. The American Psychological Association (APA) recommends a two-fold strategy of relaxation involving making a conscious effort to calm your body. First, breathe deeply. It's the old "take a deep breath and count to ten" strategy. And second, while you're breathing deeply, focus your thoughts on a calming word or phrase.[2]

Sorry, Experts, but you've stated nothing new. Thousands of years ago, the great prophet Isaiah declared, "You will keep in perfect peace all who trust in you, all *whose thoughts are fixed on you!*" (Isa. 26:3 italics added). Keeping our thoughts on the Lord has a calming effect, especially when coupled with trusting in Him. Psalm 37:7-8 also encourages relaxation. In verse 7 the psalmist instructs us to "Be still in the presence of the Lord, and wait patiently for him to act." In the next verse he says to "Stop being angry! Turn from your rage! Do not lose your temper—it only leads to harm."

Notice how verse 7's instruction provides the "how to" for verse 8's command.

Second, change the way you think—Allowing anger to go unchecked greatly impacts our thoughts. We can become irrational. That's why the APA recommends avoiding words such as "never" and "always" when thinking about yourself, someone else or a particular situation. It's easy to think you'll *never* be able to forgive or you're *always* going to hurt. These words make it difficult to think clearly and they inhibit the ability to solve problems.[3]

For months after leaving our church, I wondered how I would respond if I ran into one of the members who had caused us so much pain. I'd have imaginary conversations with them and always, I might add, I sounded eloquent. These imaginary encounters, however, only fueled my anger. To overcome them, I had to work hard at changing my thought patterns.

The apostle Paul wrote in Romans 12:2 that we are to "be transformed by the renewing of your mind" (NIV). Thankfully, the Scriptures have a lot to say about our thoughts and our minds. I'd like to offer five observations:

We must fill our minds with Scriptures. Meditation and memorization provide powerful tools for changing the way we think. Joshua commanded the children of Israel to meditate on God's Word day and night (Josh. 1:8). The psalmist wrote "Oh, the joys of those who . . . delight in the law of the Lord, meditating on it day and night" (Ps. 1:1-2). In Psalm 119:11, the psalmist said, "I have hidden your word in my heart, that I might not sin against you."

When you find yourself thinking angry thoughts or, if you're like me and you catch yourself having an imaginary conversation, start quoting Scripture and allow the power of God's Word to force out angry, bitter thoughts. Then do it again. And again. And again. Regardless of where we find ourselves in the journey of life, we will always need to focus our minds on Scriptures, day and night.

We must want our thoughts to please our heavenly Father. The late Frank Pollard, beloved pastor, theologian and seminary president, was my pastor when I was a student. Dr. Pollard, known as a gifted communicator, could pack more into a 20-minute sermon than other pastors could cover in twice that amount of time. But what I remember most about Dr. Pollard is that he concluded his prayers with Psalm 19:14: "Let the words of my mouth, and the meditation of my heart, be acceptable in thy sight, O Lord, my strength, and my redeemer" (KJV).

During my toughest days when angry thoughts bombarded my mind, I often thought of Dr. Pollard and his commitment to a mind that was pleasing to God. Many nights I'd recite Psalm 19:14 until I fell asleep. Though the battle persisted, I determined in my heart that anger would not take up permanent residence in my mind.

We must praise God. Hebrews 13:15 says "Therefore, let us offer through Jesus a continual sacrifice of praise to God, proclaiming our allegiance to his name." This requires a renewed way of thinking, especially if we're struggling with anger. If we're ever going to successfully move through anger, we must cultivate a spirit of praise. Besides, the Scriptures command us to praise God. We must praise Him if we want to live as His obedient children. You may not feel happy and joyful as you praise the Lord, but simply speaking the words of praise moves you in the right direction.

> **If we're ever going to successfully move through anger, we must cultivate a spirit of praise.**

We must express gratitude. When you're in the deepest throes of grief and anger, gratitude ranks last on your list of emotional priorities. But there's something powerful about gratitude. And, just as the Bible commands us to offer praise, it also commands us to give thanks. First Thessalonians 5:16-18 says to "Always be joyful. Never stop praying. Be thankful in all circumstances, for this is God's will for you who belong to Christ Jesus." It doesn't say we must give thanks *for* all circumstances but rather we should give thanks *in* all circumstances. Regardless of what brought us to this place of grief, we can still find something for which to be thankful. And according to Philippians 4:6-7, when we present our requests to God with thanksgiving, we will experience the peace of God that defies comprehension.

We need to take the biblical litmus test. Philippians 4:8 holds the final observation about changing the way we think. This one verse provides a litmus test for our thoughts. Are our thoughts focused on things that are true, honorable/noble, just/right, pure, lovely, admirable/commendable, excellent or praiseworthy? If not, we need to toss them out and replace them with thoughts that stand up to the litmus test.

The third step in dealing with anger is to think before you speak—This strategy comprises good old common sense and comes straight out of the New Testament. James 1:19 says, "Understand this, my dear brothers and sisters: You must all be quick to listen, slow to speak, and slow to get angry." When you find yourself moving through the element of anger, it's important that this verse become your motto. Otherwise, misdirected anger might wind up expressing itself in words that wound your children, your spouse or other innocent people.

And finally, seek help—Galatians 6:2 commands us to "Share each other's burdens, and in this way obey the law of Christ." You may find help from a friend, a co-worker or a professional counselor. The important thing is not to attempt to deal with the pain of your broken life on your own. Let's face it. We're unwilling travelers on a journey we did not choose. Anger can flare up at the most unexpected moment. One counselor described dealing with grief brought on by traumatic events to "walking through an emotional minefield." We need someone to help us process what we're going through.

Devotional Thought

If ever a man had the right to feel angry with someone it was David during his time on the run from King Saul. Why was David running from the king? Well, let's see. . . .

- ◆ David played his harp to soothe Saul whenever depression and fear overcame the king (1 Sam. 16:23).
- ◆ David served as Saul's armor bearer (1 Sam. 16:21).
- ◆ David killed Goliath, bringing victory to Saul and all Israel (1 Sam. 17:51).
- ◆ David successfully did whatever Saul asked him to do (1 Sam. 18:5).
- ◆ David skillfully led Saul's armies in battle (1 Sam. 18:16).
- ◆ Saul made plans to assassinate David (1 Sam. 19:1).

That about sums it up. David faithfully served Saul so Saul decided to kill him. We know, of course, that other factors impacted Saul's life. God had rejected Saul as king and had removed His spirit from him because of his disobedience. Saul subsequently became jealous of David's success as a soldier and his popularity among the people. And ultimately, Saul suffered from a "tormenting spirit" (1 Sam. 16:14).

David could honestly say, "I've done nothing to deserve this." Nevertheless he finds himself running for his life, hiding out in caves and commanding a ragtag army of about 600 misfit men (1 Sam. 23:13). Surely this is not what he had anticipated when the prophet Samuel anointed him. (Surely forced resignation was not what you anticipated when God called you into ministry.)

The Bible does not tell us what went through David's mind during this time, but he grappled with a host of emotions. He was human, after all. At one point he sought help from Saul's son Jonathan. "What have I done?" he exclaimed. "What is my crime?

How have I offended your father that he is so determined to kill me?" (1 Sam. 20:1).

You can literally feel the intensity of David's feelings. The specific emotions he experienced, however, are open to interpretation. Frustration? Anger? Despair? I'll let you decide.

I personally believe Saul's actions angered David. I can't help but think vivid details ran through David's mind on a never-ending loop: Saul's spear whizzing past his head on multiple occasions. Troops camped outside his own home. Climbing out a window with the help of his wife to escape Saul's men. Seeking help from the priest Ahimelech, only to have Saul find out and slaughter the man along with 84 other priests. Eighty-five holy men dead on account of one man's mission to destroy him!

And then the day came when David had the opportunity to destroy Saul. He and his men were hiding deep within a cave when Saul wandered in for a bathroom break. David's men urged him to take care of Saul once and for all. "Now's your opportunity!" they said (1 Sam. 24:4). So David crept close enough to Saul to cut off a piece of the king's robe, but he didn't harm Saul. Instead, he let him leave the cave and then, when Saul had walked some distance away David called after him. Here's what David said:

> *9Why do you listen to the people who say I am trying to harm you? 10This very day you can see with your own eyes it isn't true. For the Lord placed you at my mercy back there in the cave. Some of my men told me to kill you, but I spared you. For I said, 'I will never harm the king—he is the Lord's anointed one.' 11Look, my father, at what I have in my hand. It is a piece of the hem of your robe! I cut it off, but I didn't kill you. This proves that I am not trying to harm you and that I have not sinned against you, even though you have been hunting for me to kill me. 12May the Lord judge between us. Perhaps the Lord will punish you for what*

you are trying to do to me, but I will never harm you. (1 Sam. 24:9-12)

David had every right to be angry, but he did not act on his anger. Instead, he trusted that God would take care of matters. The Lord was judge, not David. "May the Lord judge between us," he said. "Perhaps the Lord will punish you for what you are trying to do to me," he told Saul, "but I will never harm you."

Father God, you know I am in a battle with anger and so often anger wins. You see what's in the hidden recesses of my heart. Father, you know my desire for those who have hurt us to answer for their words and deeds. Perhaps you will punish them. But perhaps not. That is up to you. Their lives are in your hands. My life is in your hands. May you judge between us.

1. "The 5 Stages of Grief." www.grief.com.

2. American Psychological Association, "Controlling Anger Before It Controls You." http://www.apa.org/topics/anger/index.aspx.

3. Ibid.

If Only
Bargaining

One of the elements of grief that has the ability to dance in and out of the other elements is bargaining. When a loved one is in a serious accident or is diagnosed with a terminal illness, it's natural to plead with God for a miracle and even to bargain with Him. "If you'll let my son live, I promise I'll never nag him about the music he listens to," or "If you'll cure my wife, I promise I'll never speak harshly to her again."

After a loved one dies, however, phase two of bargaining begins and the cries change to painful "if onlys."

If only we'd gone to the doctor sooner.

If only we'd gone to a different hospital.

If only he hadn't been running late for school.

If only it hadn't been raining.

If only . . . if only . . . if only.

This same pattern often occurs when a ministry dies. In the first phase of bargaining, the clergy couple pleads with God to make it possible for them to continue ministering at their church. With strong faith they believe God will hear their request and give them a miracle, allowing them to continue ministering to their congregation. They may even take extra precautions and might bargain with God, assuring Him they will make more hospital visits and pay more attention to the senior adults if He will come through for them on this matter. If time allows, they may even begin doing these things as a show of good faith.

After the ministry dies, however, phase two begins and they find themselves second-guessing every conversation, every committee meeting, every missed graduation celebration, every missed hospital visit. The "If Onlys" have no end. Clearly you made somebody mad and if only you could go back and do things over, maybe things would turn out differently.

Or maybe not.

The truth is, you will never know. And all of the wondering and analyzing and pondering will serve only to lead you on a downward spiral.

Wondering and analyzing and pondering will serve only to lead you on a downward spiral.

Everyone who goes through a forced exit from their church does not necessarily go through bargaining. Our exit happened so quickly that those last few days remain a blur in my memory. If I did bargain with God (I know I pleaded, but I'm not sure I promised anything in return), the bargaining lasted for only a short time. Our ministry ended so abruptly that we had no time to bargain. But the second phase, the "If Onlys," made an appearance in my grief journey periodically for quite some time. I found it hard to believe that there wasn't something we could have done to resolve the situation and avoid the painful exit.

And therein lies the hidden desire of this element of bargaining—the desire to have some control in a situation that is spinning out of control. It's the desire to fix, to solve, to heal, to make right whatever went wrong. Surely we can find an answer. Yes, we *can* find an answer. After all, God has the answer. So in desperation we cry out, "God, fix this and I'll do anything you want."

A few weeks after leaving our church, I overheard a conversation between my husband and our daughter. They were talking about the people and events that had forced our exit and our daughter asked why he had not fought to stay at the church.

Quite frankly, I wondered the same thing. We'd been in church work our entire lives and I'd known of ministers who'd chosen to

you handled that painful event. I know it wounded you deeply, but you handled everything in a Christ-like fashion and I noticed."

Spending this time alone with God has one primary purpose: ensuring that your relationship with the Father not only survives the pain but thrives during your journey of grief. You must cherish and protect your relationship with your heavenly Father above all else. What He thinks of you is all that matters. And it is only after spending time with God that we can let go of what lies behind and look forward to what lies ahead.

> **You must cherish and protect your relationship with your heavenly Father above all else.**

Devotional Thought

The bargaining element of grief can be found as far back as the Old Testament. King David tried to persuade God to save his infant son who had become gravely ill:

> [16]David pleaded with God for the child. He fasted and spent the nights lying in sackcloth on the ground. [17]The elders of his household stood beside him to get him up from the ground, but he refused, and he would not eat any food with them. [18]On the seventh day the child died. David's attendants were afraid to tell him that the child was dead, for they thought, "While the child was still living, he wouldn't listen to us when we spoke to him. How can we now tell him the child is dead? He may do something desperate." [19]David noticed that his attendants were whispering among themselves, and he realized the child was dead. "Is the child dead?" he asked. "Yes," they replied, "he is dead." [20]Then David got up from the ground. After he had washed, put on lotions and changed his clothes, he went into the house of the Lord and worshiped. Then he went to his own house, and at his request they served him food, and he ate. [21]His attendants asked him, "Why are you acting this way? While the child was alive,

you fasted and wept, but now that the child is dead, you get up and eat!" ²²*He answered, "While the child was still alive, I fasted and wept. I thought, 'Who knows? The Lord may be gracious to me and let the child live.'"* (2 Sam. 12:16-22 NIV)

Who knows, indeed? And so we pray. We plead. We may even try to bargain. But in the end, regardless of whether or not God steps in and saves the day, it is our obedience to Him and to His Word that matters.

Understanding why God allows some of His servants' lives to be shattered by their own congregations is beyond me. But many times throughout my journey of grief I have been reminded of my Father's words in Isaiah 55:8-9: "For my thoughts are not your thoughts, neither are your ways my ways," declares the Lord. "As the heavens are higher than the earth, so are my ways higher than your ways and my thoughts than your thoughts."

Father God, I don't understand why you have allowed our lives to be shattered. I have begged and I have pleaded. Now I give up. I don't understand, but then again, I don't have to understand. I simply must obey. So Father, forgive me but I need to bargain with you one last time. Here's what I promise: if you will give me the strength to obey you, I will obey. But you have to provide the strength, Father, because I simply can't do this on my own.

Slogging Through the Fog
Depression

When our ministry died abruptly, my sister-in-law encouraged me to visit my doctor and get a prescription for an anti-depressant. I stubbornly refused. I reasoned that God would give me whatever I needed to make it through the days ahead. I would pray without ceasing. I would consider it all joy. I would cast my cares on the Lord. I would do all things through Christ who gave me strength.

What I did not take into consideration was the impact a traumatic event has on a body, both physically and physiologically. While many degrees of depression exist ranging from mild non-clinical to severe clinical—and I do not pretend to even scratch the surface of addressing these in this chapter—one generally accepted theory is that a chemical imbalance can bring on depression. And suffering a traumatic event such as the loss of a loved one or the loss of a job can trigger this imbalance. The trigger does double damage for clergy couples who suffer the loss of people they love while simultaneously losing their ministry.

As an element of grief, depression quietly descends upon those who grieve, enveloping them in murky fog that lifts and resettles with little warning. Avoiding it borders on the impossible. If you feel depressed, count yourself among those who experience a normal and appropriate response to great loss. When a traumatic event causes depression, it doesn't mean you're weak. It doesn't mean your faith is small. It doesn't mean you have a mental illness. It means life has dealt you a harsh

Depression quietly descends upon those who grieve, enveloping them in murky fog that lifts and resettles with little warning.

blow—one that has knocked you flat and the mere task of breathing presents a painful challenge.

The harsh blow of forced resignation led me down a dark path of sadness that subtly merged into the dense fog of depression. All hope seemed gone. I found myself suspended in time between the life I had once enjoyed and the life that had yet to unfold. I often found myself staring into space while everything around me moved in slow motion. Little voices whispered, "This is it. Get used to it. Life isn't going to get any better. You're never going to experience happiness again."

You may exhibit other symptoms of depression:

♦ You cry more than usual and often at something completely insignificant.
♦ You feel as though you're suffocating, drowning or moving through fog.
♦ Everything seems hopeless.
♦ You're worried all the time.
♦ You feel like you can't do anything right.
♦ You have difficulty making the simplest decision.
♦ You find it hard to concentrate.
♦ You can't sleep or you sleep too much.

Please note, this is not an exhaustive list of the symptoms of depression. And one key symptom is not addressed at all—that of suicidal thoughts. **If you have recurring thoughts of death or suicide, put down this book and seek professional help immediately.** *There's nothing to be ashamed of. You're simply in over your head. But you're not alone!*

There's nothing to be ashamed of. You're simply in over your head.

If any of this sounds familiar to you, take heart. The great prophet Elijah knew exactly what you're going through. Theologians have described him as a rugged individualist and a fearless reformer. He had an extraordinary ministry filled with divine power and drama. He stood before kings, infuriated queens and called down fire from heaven. Yet Elijah came to a point where he was running for his life. Literally. He felt dejected and alone. It was just him and a scrawny tree. So he lay down under the tree, asked God to let him die and went to sleep, hoping never to awaken.

Throughout the months when I felt trapped in depression, I identified with Elijah. I felt isolated and completely alone. I stopped short of asking God to let me die but I begged Him to end the pain. I was so tired of hurting and even more tired of watching my husband hurt. Nothing made sense. The pain. The loneliness. The isolation. They were interminable, and even though I knew what the Scriptures promised, it felt like God had deserted us. I remember on several occasions lying in the dark in the middle of a sleepless night, staring at the foot of the bed and pleading with Jesus to appear. I desperately wanted to see Him with my eyes, to hear Him with my ears as He assured me I would survive.

As I look at the story of Elijah now with a clearer perspective, the thing that stands out to me is not that a great man of God struggled with depression. What amazes me is God's response to Elijah's depression. God didn't scold Elijah for wanting to die. He didn't shower him with a barrage of pious platitudes. Instead, He sent an angel to minister to him. Under the angel's care, Elijah woke up, had a bite to eat and went back to sleep. We're not told how long Elijah slept, but eventually the angel woke him up and instructed him to eat again because "the journey is too much for you" (1 Kings 19:7 NIV).

I really like this angel. For one thing, he acknowledged the difficulty of Elijah's situation. He offered no pat answers nor did he spout off the latest positive thinking strategy. Instead, he encouraged the great prophet to eat because "the journey is too much for you." The angel also touched Elijah each time he awakened him. Throughout the Bible, angels are said to have appeared to or gone to Gideon, Samson's mother, Joseph, Zechariah and Mary (Judg.

6:12 and 13:3; Matt. 1:20; Luke 1:11, 28). And an angel wrestled with Jacob (Gen. 32:24). But the angel touched Elijah. In fact, while angels play an active role throughout both the Old and New Testaments, 1 Kings 19 is the only place where an angel is said to have touched the person he appeared to. That's incredible! Almighty God, through the angel, reached down from heaven and touched Elijah in his depression.

Touch is powerful. Something as simple as an arm around your shoulder can give enormous comfort and strength. The problem for couples whose ministries have ended is that we may have a small number of people left who will offer the needed touch. Our families lived over 500 miles away. My best friend lived twice that distance. My husband and I had only each other, so we touched more often than usual. We held hands or I'd slip my arm through his. Our legs would touch when we sat on the sofa. Our arms would touch when we worshiped in mega churches where no one knew us. And we hugged. A lot. My arms wrapped around his waist, his around my shoulders. We were keeping each other from falling completely to pieces and we knew it.

But back to Elijah. God sent an angel to minister to Elijah and, once Elijah regained his strength, the journey continued. And never once did God reprimand him for getting depressed. So when you find yourself moving in and out and back into the element of depression, recognize it as a normal part of your journey through grief and be gentle with yourself. Allow God to minister to you in whatever way He chooses.

> **Recognize depression as a normal part of your journey through grief and be gentle with yourself.**

And please, make an appointment with your doctor. Tell him or her what you're going through and what you're feeling. Together with your doctor you can make a decision about how to best handle this element of your grief. My sister-in-law recommended doing this and I didn't heed her advice, but I wish I had. Months later, when I couldn't make it through a day without sobbing, my body forced me to seek help. Working through the element of depression was challenging, but it might not have been as intense had I visited with my doctor when my journey of grief first began.

Devotional Thought

Even though the term "depression" is not often found in the Scriptures, references to the symptoms of depression are plentiful.

When Nehemiah learned that the wall of Jerusalem had fallen and the gates had been burned, he "wept" and "mourned." When he approached Artaxerxes, the king asked, "Why are you sad, when you aren't sick? This is nothing but depression" (Neh. 2:2 HCSB). Moses became despondent while trying to lead the children of Israel and told God, "If this is how you intend to treat me, just go ahead and kill me. Do me a favor and spare me this misery!" (Num. 11:15). At one point, Jeremiah was so depressed that he cried out, "Oh, that I had died at birth!" (Jer. 15:10). And in his intense suffering, Job said, "I hate my life and don't want to go on living" (Job 7:16).

And then there's David. Psalm 6:6-7 describes him as "worn out by sobbing" and "his vision blurred by grief." He has cried so much that his tears have drenched his bed. In Psalm 143:7 he cries out for the Lord to answer him "for my depression deepens." And in Psalm 13:1-3, David asks, "O Lord, how long will you forget me? Forever? How long will you look the other way? How long must I struggle with anguish in my soul, with sorrow in my heart every day? How long will my enemy have the upper hand? Turn and answer me, O Lord my God! Restore the sparkle to my eyes, or I will die."

Even Jesus, who knew how His story would end, felt so alone on the cross that He cried out, "My God, my God, why have you abandoned me?" (Matt. 27:45-46).

If you're struggling with immense sadness and feel completely alone, you're in good company. Such depression, whether experienced briefly or for longer periods of time, is inevitable when facing great loss.

Father God, I desperately want this depression to end. I want to have a song in my heart rather than a cloud in my soul. Though at times I cannot feel your presence, I'm holding on to your promise that you will never leave me. By sheer faith, I trust that you will eventually take me through this dreary fog and into your everlasting light.

Coming to Grips with Reality
Acceptance

I placed my trust in God today,
For it is He who knows the way,
And when uncertainties arise,
I trust His judgment, true and wise.
I'll place my trust in God today,
Even when I cannot see the way,
He'll lead me on with His strong hand,
Until I reach the promised land.
("I Place My Trust in God," public domain)

The words from this old hymn beautifully illustrate my experience in the element of acceptance. This element is not about saying "Everything's OK." Quite frankly, what a couple experiences when they are forced to leave their church can never be described as OK. The element of acceptance is about letting go of the loss and coming to grips with the new reality that has become your life. The element of acceptance means you're able to say, "Ok, this is my reality. I don't like it, it's not fair, it's not right, but here I am. Now what?"

Acceptance is about letting go of the loss and coming to grips with the new reality that has become your life.

It's important to note that even though acceptance always appears as the last element of grief, it does not signal that all of the other elements have been resolved. In fact, I moved through the element of acceptance long before the elements of anger and depression began to diminish.

When a ministry couple faces forced resignation, many questions must be answered. *How will you survive financially? How will you find another job? Do you even want to stay in church work? If not, what will you do? If you do want to stay in church work, how will you get another church to consider you? How will you answer their questions regarding why you left your previous church? If you own your home, should you sell and move elsewhere? If you have children living at home, how will these events impact their lives? How will the events impact the lives of your children who are grown?*

Within days of leaving our church, my husband felt that God had released him from his call to pastor. That's not to say God told him he should not pastor, simply that he had fulfilled his calling. My husband didn't have any idea what lay ahead for us, nor did I, but he felt God had given him permission to pursue work other than pastoring a local church. Over the next few months, I continued working at my job as he began the painstaking ordeal of job hunting. The nation was in the middle of the worst recession since the Great Depression and it didn't take long to discover firsthand that no one was hiring. As the weeks and months wore on with no hope of a new job, we came to one conclusion—we wanted to go home. We desperately needed to surround ourselves with people who loved us. It was time to move back to our home state and live close to our families. From there we would continue to search for God's direction and rebuild our lives.

Throughout the months since our world had shattered, we'd faithfully prayed for guidance. We pleaded with God to show us what to do. But God seemed unusually quiet. All my life I'd heard people talk about times of grief when, even in their darkest hour, they knew God's presence. Some even declared they experienced a greater closeness to God during their grief than they'd ever known before. I regarded these people with jealous skepticism because I couldn't detect God's presence anywhere. But we continued to pray for wisdom. We continued to ask God what we should do. When clear direction didn't come, we eventually began asking Him to keep us from making a wrong decision rather than asking Him to help us make the right one.

When we finally determined it was time to put our house on the market, we had no idea what to expect. We just knew we had to sell before we could move closer to our families. The housing market had all but died, with the foreclosure rate reaching an all-time high, but we had no choice. We had to sell. We couldn't afford to keep the house with my income alone and, even if we could, we didn't want to stay in the area. There were too many memories and too much pain. So we painted the house, cleaned the carpets, and sold anything we didn't want to pack and move. Then we met with a realtor and put the house on the market. Most houses were staying on the market for months, some for over a year the realtor said. So we waited.

We didn't have long to wait. Our house sold for the asking price within 5 weeks. For the first time in months I could see God's hand in our lives. My dear father-in-law invited us to live with him until we found jobs, so as soon as we finalized the sale of the house I resigned my job, we packed everything we owned and headed home to family. My husband drove the rental truck and I followed behind.

As I drove along the interstate staring at the back of the rental, I couldn't help but think of a figurine we'd purchased thirty years earlier, now nestled in bubble wrap and packed in one of the boxes marked "Fragile" deep within the truck. The figurine, entitled "Walking by Faith," depicts a young husband pulling a cart piled high with household goods; perched on top of the pile sits his young wife. As I drove behind the truck that held all of our worldly possessions, I knew without any doubt we were walking by faith. We had no home, no jobs, and nothing on the horizon. All we could do was put one foot in front of the other, believing God would see us through.

A full moon shone brightly by the time we pulled up in front of my father-in-law's home. Exhaustion consumed me but adrenaline surged through my body as a host of emotions began surfacing. An incongruous mixture of gratitude, anger, fear and relief spilled out of my pores as I began unloading the car. I could faintly hear the sound of my husband's voice in the distance, pleading with me to slow down. But I knew if I slowed down I might stop, and if I stopped I would surely fall apart. So I forged ahead, determined to carry in every box, every suitcase and every armload of clothes until finally my car sat empty.

Then I stopped.

And then I fell apart.

Through my tears I found myself standing in my father-in-law's guest room. I couldn't believe that in a blur of time I had gone from living in a beautiful multi-level home that was mine to living in one room that belonged to someone else. We didn't know it at the time, but that room would be our home for the next seven months. Seven long months.

During this time we became involved with two groups that provided strength and encouragement. The first was a job search support group made up of several hundred unemployed professionals. In a way, the group was an example of the old adage "misery loves company." Every Tuesday we'd meet for several hours to network with other people facing similar challenges and attend workshops on job searching in the digital age. We'd celebrate the news of those who'd found employment and secretly wish we had landed the job instead.

The second group my husband and I found was a congregation of about two hundred people not far from my father-in-law's house. On the one hand, attending the church would be dangerous because we'd stand out as visitors in such a small congregation. Up until this point, we'd attended mega churches, not for the worship experience but for the ability to be invisible. Attending a smaller church took courage, but we figured we didn't have to go back if we didn't want to, so one Sunday we took a few deep breaths and went. The experience proved one of the best decisions we'd made in our journey, for we found a group of loving people who welcomed us with open arms. We had anticipated questions like "Are you new to the area?" and "Do you live around here?" so we had carefully crafted our answer: "We're transitioning back to this area and are looking for jobs." That's all we told people and, thankfully, they didn't pry. When we returned the next Sunday, a couple who sat nearby greeted us like old friends. They had a gift for making us feel loved without needing to know our background. Over the next several months, they'd ask about our job search, our kids and our plans for Christmas—questions about the future but never about the past. Because of this dear couple, we had a place to worship where we felt we belonged. A place where, if we were absent, someone noticed.

The church where we worshipped for several months played a vital role in my ability to move through the element of acceptance. As I look back now, several other things stand out as balms that made this particular element more bearable.

You're probably expecting me to list prayer and Bible study as balms through this difficult time so I'll start with those. Yes, there's no question that prayer and Bible study provided the necessary nourishment to keep my soul alive. Thanks to my sister-in-law, I found a women's Bible study at a church that met in a movie theater. We'd sneak in the back of the theater just as the video started and slip out as soon as the credits began to roll. I was not ready to share my heart with other women in small discussion groups, but I felt like I'd achieved a milestone each time I made it through the video without becoming an emotional mess.

Reading provided another balm that made life more bearable. My father-in-law got me hooked on a series of suspense thrillers that, to this day, has me cheering for the protagonist because of his deep sense of justice. When he sees a wrong, he makes it right. He might break some bones and blow up half the county in the process, but he doesn't put up with bad guys mistreating good guys. He became my hero, even if he was fictitious.

It doesn't take a degree in psychology to understand why I got hooked on such a protagonist. When your life is shattered because of other people's actions and you're suffering pain more intense than you ever imagined possible, the thought of someone coming to your defense and making your enemies pay for what they've done. . . well . . . it's an awfully nice thought. When Christ returns, Satan will pay for all the evil he's done and that will be a glorious day. But in the meantime, I wanted those who'd caused us so much pain to pay. I wanted some justice here on earth. And since that's not the way things happened, reading novels where the protagonist comes to town and makes the bad guys pay became a catharsis for me.

Laughter provided another great balm for moving through the element of acceptance. Quite frankly, when we moved into my father-in-law's house, I didn't feel like laughing. But I soon learned that laughter was one of my father-in-law's greatest qualities. Until we lived with him, I never realized just how much he laughs. At least once a day I'd hear belly laughs coming from the family room where he watched his favorite television shows. He never tried to make me laugh, nor did he insist I watch a sitcom with him so I'd cheer up. He just went about his day and showed me by example the importance of laughter. Eventually his laughter drew me in and I began watching some of his shows with him. Solomon was right: A cheerful heart really is good medicine.

Perhaps the greatest balm for my journey through acceptance came through music. Not all music provided a balm though. One CD in particular caused a stinging pain like pouring salt into an open wound. Before our forced resignation, this particular CD had been one of my favorites—Christmas carols with piano and handbells. I loved handbells and I'd played in many bell choirs since my college days. In fact, I still remember the last handbell rehearsal I attended, four days before being forced to leave our church. From that day on, the sound of handbells only intensified my grief.

But other music provided a wonderful balm. Music has always played an enormous role in my life and it became even more important in my journey of grief. Lyrics to old hymns as well as contemporary Christian songs became my own prayers. "It Is Well with My Soul" and "Great Is Thy Faithfulness" provided immense comfort; and the lyrics of artists like Third Day, MIKESCHAIR, Matt Maher and Casting Crowns became my own prayers. I found strength knowing others had felt the same intense emotions I was feeling. And when my thoughts and emotions jumbled to the point I couldn't express my mind and heart, I was grateful to discover someone else had done it for me.

I found strength knowing others had felt the same intense emotions I was feeling.

This same attitude applies to many of the psalms. I think that's why so many people who grieve find comfort in the psalmist's words. When we can't express what is in our heart, the psalmist does it for us.

Devotional Thought

Psalm 40 could be the theme song of those who find themselves in the element of acceptance. See if you can identify with the psalmist's words:

> [1]*I waited patiently for the LORD to help me,*
> *and he turned to me and heard my cry.*
> [2]*He lifted me out of the pit of despair,*
> *out of the mud and the mire.*
> *He set my feet on solid ground*
> *and steadied me as I walked along.*

³He has given me a new song to sing,
a hymn of praise to our God.
Many will see what he has done and be amazed.
They will put their trust in the Lord.

David began this psalm by reflecting on a painful time in his life when he cried out to God for help. We're not told which of David's turbulent life moments inspired this psalm, but clearly it was a time of intense suffering and pain. Whatever the circumstances, they had landed him in "the pit of despair." The description of being in mud and mire indicates his inability to get himself out of the pit. It was slippery and slimy, and on those occasions when David had surely attempted to get himself out of the dark hole, he slid right back down into despair.

While skidding around in the pit, David cried out to the Lord and "waited patiently" for the Lord to come to his aid. The fact that David "waited patiently" indicates God did not answer immediately. After all, we need patience only when we have to wait. But after a period of time, God lifted David out of the pit, set his feet on solid ground and steadied him as he walked.

I love the imagery of God steadying David as he walked along. Who knows how long David had spent in the muddy, slimy pit, suffering intense hardship and pain. Beaten, battered and bruised David was worn out. It was going to take awhile to regain his strength. And until he did, God steadied him.

Beaten, battered, bruised, unsteady on my feet. By the time I accepted that my life would never be the same, those words described me to a T. And, like David, God picked me up out of the pit and steadied me until I grew stronger.

A part of you has been amputated. It will take time for the healing to begin and to regain your strength.

Perhaps that's where you find yourself right now. Beaten and bruised. If so, be gentle with yourself and allow God to steady you. You've been through a major surgery. A part of you has been amputated. It will take time for the healing to begin and to regain your strength. Lean on the Lord and allow Him to steady you as you grow stronger.

Reflecting on this experience of God's deliverance prompted David to burst into praise. Indeed, the memory of what God had done in the past gave David a new reason to praise God in the present.

> *⁴Oh, the joys of those who trust the LORD,*
> *who have no confidence in the proud*
> *or in those who worship idols.*
> *⁵O LORD my God, you have performed many wonders for us.*
> *Your plans for us are too numerous to list.*
> *You have no equal.*
> *If I tried to recite all your wonderful deeds,*
> *I would never come to the end of them.*

Remembering the depths of his despair reminded David of the greatness of his God. Looking back at the pit, he saw how far God had brought him. David praised God for His "many wonders"— those times when God had intervened and delivered David in times of trouble.

And oh, how I love the next line: "Your plans for us are too numerous to list." God has a plan for each of our lives. He takes every part of life—the beautiful and the ugly—and works it into His plan for us as only He can do. It wasn't until I experienced the acceptance element of grief that I truly began to grasp God's ability to use ugliness to bring about beauty, even though ugliness was not part of His original plan.

> *⁶You take no delight in sacrifices or offerings.*
> *Now that you have made me listen, I finally understand—*
> *you don't require burnt offerings or sin offerings.*
> *⁷Then I said, "Look, I have come.*

As is written about me in the Scriptures:
[8]I take joy in doing your will, my God,
for your instructions are written on my heart."

A major part of the acceptance element for me required coming to the point where I could truly say, "I take joy in doing your will, my God." I easily proclaimed these words when I was a pastor's wife and life made sense. But afterwards, when I grieved so deeply for a life that was gone, finding joy in doing God's will—especially when I no longer knew what doing His will meant—proved challenging. Getting to the point where I could say, "I will take joy in doing your will, whatever that may be," was a long process.

[9]I have told all your people about your justice.
I have not been afraid to speak out,
as you, O Lord, well know.
[10]I have not kept the good news of your justice hidden in my heart;
I have talked about your faithfulness and saving power.
I have told everyone in the great assembly
of your unfailing love and faithfulness.

Just as David wanted to tell others about God's faithfulness and His unfailing love, I want to tell wounded clergy couples about God's faithfulness and His miraculous power to use evil for good. You, too, will have your story to tell. Though you may doubt it now, the day will come when you will be able to say, "God delivered me from the pit of despair. His love and faithfulness never failed."

[11]Lord, don't hold back your tender mercies from me.
Let your unfailing love and faithfulness always protect me.
[12]For troubles surround me—
too many to count!
My sins pile up so high

I can't see my way out.
They outnumber the hairs on my head.
I have lost all courage.
¹³Please, LORD, rescue me!
Come quickly, LORD, and help me.
¹⁴May those who try to destroy me
be humiliated and put to shame.
May those who take delight in my trouble
be turned back in disgrace.
¹⁵Let them be horrified by their shame,
for they said, "Aha! We've got him now!"
¹⁶But may all who search for you
be filled with joy and gladness in you.
May those who love your salvation
repeatedly shout, "The LORD is great!"
¹⁷As for me, since I am poor and needy,
let the Lord keep me in his thoughts.
You are my helper and my savior.
O my God, do not delay.

In the final section of Psalm 40, David prayed for future deliverance. He knew "troubles" are a part of life. He would need God's protection and help to withstand the people who wanted to destroy him. So David prayed urgently for God's deliverance: "Rescue me." "Come quickly." "O my God, do not delay."

Although David opened this psalm with "I waited patiently for the Lord to help me," he ended it with "O my God, do not delay." Both attitudes are right and pleasing to God.

When trouble arises and we're faced with painful circumstances, it's only natural to cry out to God for speedy deliverance. We are His children, the sheep of His pasture. He wants us to turn to Him for help. And sometimes He answers quickly, without delay.

But sometimes, for reasons known only to God, He delays. And sometimes, God hears our cry and immediately answers but the answer is delayed in reaching us. Consider the account in Daniel 10 where Daniel had been involved in an extended period of fervent prayer, desperately seeking an answer from God. Finally, after being delayed, God's messenger arrived:

> [12]*Then he said, "Don't be afraid, Daniel. Since the first day you began to pray for understanding and to humble yourself before your God, your request has been heard in heaven. I have come in answer to your prayer.* [13]*But for twenty-one days the spirit prince of the kingdom of Persia blocked my way. Then Michael, one of the archangels, came to help me, and I left him there with the spirit prince of the kingdom of Persia.* [14]*Now I am here to explain what will happen to your people in the future, for this vision concerns a time yet to come."*

James 5:16 tells us "The earnest prayer of a righteous person has great power and produces wonderful results." But sometimes we don't realize what that "power" involves. While prayer is conversation with God, it is a spiritual conversation, a conversation that takes place in the spirit world. And as we see in Daniel, the powers of evil have the ability to hinder and delay the answers to our prayers. Just as God has given free will to humans, He has given free will and limited powers to demons. Spiritual warfare is real, it is powerful, and its impact is far-reaching. God can overrule the powers of Satan anytime He chooses, and we look forward to the day when Christ returns and demonstrates His victory over evil. But until that day comes, evil will impact our lives. Sometimes we stare evil in the face, and other times evil affects us in the heavenly realms where spiritual battles continually wage.

Two things stand out to me in Daniel 10. The first is that angels and demons are fighting spiritual battles on my behalf even though most of the time I am completely unaware of them. I cannot see what is taking place in the heavenly realms but the activity exists nonetheless.

The second thing that stands out to me is that God answers prayer, even if the answer gets delayed in reaching me. I'm not saying every time I have to wait for an answer from God that there is a demon fighting to keep the answer from me. I have no way of knowing what causes the delay. But it helps to remember there's a lot going on in the spirit world about which I have no knowledge.

And that brings me to a concluding thought. As I have traveled this journey of grief I have come to embrace the freedom that comes with saying, "I don't know." I don't know why, I don't know what, I don't know how and I don't know when. But I do know God. And knowing Him is enough.

Father God, I don't know why we have to hurt so deeply, but I trust you, Lord, to heal our pain. I don't know what lies ahead for us, but I trust you, Lord, to guide us. I don't know how we're going to pay for a mortgage, for college, for medical bills. But I trust you, Lord, to provide. I don't know when life will feel stable again, but I trust you, Lord, to steady us. I don't know where we're going to land, but I trust you, Lord, to be there with us and to never, ever forsake us.

PART TWO

THE JOURNEY CONTINUES

Praying in Grief

Parenting in Grief

The Power of Response

Epilogue

Praying in Grief

Eloquent will never be the adjective of choice to describe my prayers. I've always just dumped out my heart to God. Adoration, confession, thanksgiving and supplication tumble out in random order. And in the darkest days of my grief, prayers of supplication dominated my prayer life. Often I simply uttered one word: *Help.*

For the brief period of time between the moment we learned anything was wrong and our resignation, we prayed fervently for our church family. We prayed for wisdom. We prayed for God's protection of innocent bystanders—those whose spiritual lives would be deeply hurt by conflict within the church. We prayed for the miracle of healing. We prayed that people would open their eyes to see the truth. And we prayed in faith, believing God would answer. I leaned heavily on 2 Chronicles 20:15 where King Jehoshaphat heard these encouraging words: "Do not be afraid or discouraged because of this vast army. For the battle is not yours, but God's" (NIV). The entire twentieth chapter of 2 Chronicles had encouraged and strengthened me on numerous occasions and I firmly believed God was going to fight this battle for us.

To this day, I do not understand why God answered our prayers as He did. Perhaps His answer is still unfolding. I do not know. What I do know is that innocent people were hurt, relationships were not healed, and people still do not know the truth. We stood firm in our faith, believing He was going to fight the battle. But instead of truth and healing, we were obliterated. I am not blaming God. I am simply acknowledging that I do not understand why He allowed events to play out as they did. I know the circumstances that unfolded involved free will and sin, but I don't understand why God did not step in and change the outcome. He could have done so but He chose not to.

During the weeks and months following our resignation, my faith was shaken to the core. Where was God? What was He doing? I desperately wanted to believe He had a new plan for our lives, but I barely had the strength to make it through one day, much less consider what might be awaiting us in the future. The grief that so enveloped me sapped every ounce of energy, leaving me completely exhausted.

In many ways, I was like the paralyzed man in Mark 2 who couldn't get himself to Jesus. Four of his friends, determined to get him to the feet of the Savior, carried him on his mat to the house where Jesus was teaching. When they couldn't get through the door because of the crowd, they cut a hole in the roof and lowered him to the feet of the Great Physician. The Bible says Jesus healed the paralyzed man because of his friends' faith (v. 5).

One of the things that carried me through the long months of grief was a group of "mat bearers" committed to getting me to Jesus. My "mat bearers" were members of my best friend's Bible class three states away. They didn't know me, but they faithfully lowered me to the feet of Jesus week after week as they prayed for God's comfort, strength and healing. On those days when grief paralyzed my mind and spirit, these "mat bearers" prayed for me, and Jesus answered their prayers for me because of their faith.

As months passed and our journey of grief grew darker, I found it increasingly difficult to find hope as I prayed. There had been too many job leads that led nowhere, phone calls that were never returned. I felt suspended in time with the past firmly closed and the future yet to open. I struggled with Psalm 5:3 where David wrote, "Listen to my voice in the morning, Lord. Each morning I bring my requests to you and wait expectantly."

> I felt suspended in time with the past firmly closed and the future yet to open.

Really, David? You wait expectantly day after day? I mean, sure, at the very beginning my faith was strong and I believed God's answer was just around the corner. But week after week and month after month of watching my husband grieve left me discouraged. I just couldn't bring my requests to God each morning and then wait expectantly throughout the day.

It was during this time that I read of a man who'd battled a rare disease for several years. He and his wife had prayed for healing. They never doubted God could heal him, but after three years of what appeared to be unanswered prayer, he was tired. He said it was "too exhausting" to sustain an attitude of "expectation."[1]

That's exactly how I felt. I simply could not sustain an attitude of expectation. So how should I pray? Should I follow the example of the persistent widow in Luke 18 who kept pleading with the judge until he finally gave her what she asked of him? Should I bring my burdens to the Lord and "leave them there" as the old hymn says? Finding a balance between Jesus' teaching to "Keep on asking, and you will receive what you ask for" (Matt. 7:7) and Peter's admonition to "Cast all your anxiety on him because he cares for you" (1 Pet. 5:7 NIV) proved to be a challenge.

Looking back, it's clear I have prayed many different types of prayer throughout my journey of grief. But the one that stands out over the others is what Richard Foster refers to as the Prayer of Relinquishment in his book *Prayer: Finding the Heart's True Home*.[2] Praying this type of prayer did not come easily, by any means. The Prayer of Relinquishment has its roots in the Garden of Gethsemane, a place of anguish and pain. In Matthew 26:38 we read where Jesus told His disciples, "My soul is crushed with grief to the point of death." He did not want to suffer the crucifixion and He pleaded with the Father to spare Him the events that were about to happen. In fact, Jesus repeatedly asked the Father if there wasn't some way to avoid humiliation and death. Ultimately, though, His struggle in the garden led to relinquishment: "Yet I want your will to be done, not mine" (v. 39).

The ability to pray this prayer and truly mean it was a process for me. At first, as I struggled with anger and depression, my prayers were not true relinquishment, even though my words echoed Jesus' prayer in Gethsemane. My words were right but my heart wasn't. The attitude of my heart was fatalism, not relinquishment. I had resigned myself to the fact that if this was what God wanted for us, so be it.

But fatalism smacks of a God who is distant and uninvolved in the lives of His children—a God who put our lives in motion at the time of our birth and then just walked away. And that does not describe the God of the Bible. The God of the Bible exudes love and mercy, goodness and wisdom. The God of the Bible has promised He will never forsake His children. The God of the Bible would never put our lives in motion and abandon us to spin out of control.

The God of the Bible would never put our lives in motion and abandon us to spin out of control.

Relinquishment, on the other hand, involves conversation with God as we seek His direction for our future. It's a process of working *with* God to impact how our life unfolds. Rather than being fatalistic, God wants us to share our hopes and dreams with Him. He wants us to work *with* Him, all the while acknowledging that He is in control.

During the weeks and months following our resignation, we claimed James 1:5 and continually prayed for wisdom and direction. "If you need wisdom, ask our generous God, and he will give it to you. He will not rebuke you for asking." So many decisions had to be made but we were in no shape to make them. We were starting over, rebuilding our lives and desperately seeking God's will. What did He want us to do? Surely He had a place for us to invest our lives, didn't He? But what was it? Where was it? As we prayed, we trusted God to give wisdom. We did not feel His direction, but we trusted it was there.

Praying through times of grief involves many kinds of prayer. In the darkest moments, Romans 8:26 assured me I didn't have to know the right words to pray because "the Holy Spirit prays for us with groanings that cannot be expressed in words." I clung to this verse on those days when I couldn't form a sentence, much less pray a coherent prayer.

I must admit that through much of my journey of grief, I wanted God to explain Himself. Why had He allowed our lives to be blown apart? Why had He allowed evil to win? God never gave me the explanation I wanted anymore than He gave an explanation to Job. The fact is, I would not have understood His explanation had He chosen to give one. God's thoughts and ways are far beyond what I will ever be able to understand.

When our daughter was an infant, she had terrible colic. Our pediatrician assured us she would outgrow it and in the meantime all we could really do was hold her. Night after night I'd walk the floor, holding my precious little baby in my arms as she wailed in pain. One night I noticed her tiny hands clenching the fabric of my shirt as though if she let go she would surely fall. I remember thinking, "Oh my child, my arms are wrapped around you. You're not going anywhere. Relax, little one. I'm not letting go of you." I couldn't explain to her why she hurt. I could have spoken the words, but she would never have been able to comprehend the explanation. All I could do was hold on to her in the midst of her pain.

Throughout my journey of grief, my heavenly Father has had His arms wrapped around me, holding tightly through the long nights of my wailing and pain. But had He chosen to give me an explanation for His allowing our suffering, I would no more have been able to understand it than my infant daughter would have understood my explanation of colic. God's ways are not my ways. His thoughts are not my thoughts. He is God.

Like many couples who have faced forced resignation, I found great solace in the prayers of the Psalms. One minister's wife told me God gave her Psalm 118:6-7 during her journey of grief: "The Lord is with me; I will not be afraid. What can mere mortals do to me? The Lord is with me; he is my helper. I look in triumph on my enemies" (NIV). Her husband also found solace in the Psalms. "I watched him struggle with his pain and the reality of where we were, wondering what to do next. For over 38 years he had been a minister and I a minister's wife. Now he was thinking of leaving the ministry. He would sit and read the Bible for hours. The Psalms were a comfort to him," she said.

It's no wonder clergy couples who grieve often find comfort in the Psalms. Many of these literary masterpieces expose the anguish of a soul shattered by betrayal. Second Samuel 15 sets the stage for the raw emotions found in many of David's poems. It's a story many couples can identify with all too well.

> [1]*After this, Absalom bought a chariot and horses, and he hired fifty bodyguards to run ahead of him.* [2]*He got up early every morning and went out to the gate of the city. When people brought a case to the king for judgment, Absalom would ask where in Israel they were from, and they would tell him their tribe.* [3]*Then Absalom would say, "You've really got a strong case here! It's too bad the king doesn't have anyone to hear it.* [4]*I wish I were the judge. Then everyone could bring their cases to me for judgment, and I would give them justice!"*
> [5]*When people tried to bow before him, Absalom wouldn't let them. Instead, he took them by the hand and kissed them.* [6]*Absalom did this with everyone who came to the king for judgment, and so he stole the hearts of all the people of Israel.*
> [7]*After four years, Absalom said to the king, "Let me go to Hebron to offer a sacrifice to the Lord and fulfill a vow I made to him.* [8]*For*

while your servant was at Geshur in Aram, I promised to sacrifice
to the Lord in Hebron if he would bring me back to Jerusalem."
⁹"All right," the king told him. "Go and fulfill your vow."
So Absalom went to Hebron. ¹⁰But while he was there, he sent
secret messengers to all the tribes of Israel to stir up a rebel-
lion against the king. "As soon as you hear the ram's horn,"
his message read, "you are to say, 'Absalom has been crowned
king in Hebron.'" ¹¹He took 200 men from Jerusalem with him as
guests, but they knew nothing of his intentions. ¹²While Absalom
was offering the sacrifices, he sent for Ahithophel, one of David's
counselors who lived in Giloh. Soon many others also joined
Absalom, and the conspiracy gained momentum. ¹³A messenger
soon arrived in Jerusalem to tell David, "All Israel has joined
Absalom in a conspiracy against you!" (2 Sam. 15:1-13)

Much of the grief found in the psalms is rooted in Absalom's betrayal of his father. What is so frightening, and the reason Absalom's betrayal worked so well, is that it was so subtle. He didn't storm the king's palace to overthrow his father. He didn't arm himself with arrows and swords. No, his weapon was more powerful than that. His weapon was conversation. His arsenal was stocked with words.

Had Absalom tried to storm the palace, David's men would have stopped him in a heartbeat. But that wasn't his plan. Instead, he hung around the city gates and talked to people as they arrived with problems that needed the king's wisdom and sound judgment. With carefully chosen words, a strong handshake and an understanding arm around the shoulder, Absalom planted seeds of doubt regarding his father's competence. Absalom calculated every word and every action to win the people's hearts away from his father. Slowly. Subtly. Subversively.

And it worked.

After four years of sowing seeds of discord, Absalom made his move. "All Israel has joined Absalom in a conspiracy against you!" the messenger cried.

Absalom calculated every word and every action to win the people's hearts away from his father. Slowly. Subtly. Subversively.

One moment. One messenger. And David's life was shattered. Initially, his military training kicked in and he made the decisions necessary to save his life and the lives of his family members. But eventually, the pain of betrayal demanded attention and David grieved.

How long will you people ruin my reputation? How long will you make groundless accusations? How long will you continue your lies? (Ps. 4:2)

My enemies cannot speak a truthful word. Their deepest desire is to destroy others. (Ps. 5:9a)

I am losing all hope; I am paralyzed with fear. (Ps. 143:4)

Come quickly, Lord, and answer me, for my depression deepens. Don't turn away from me, or I will die. (Ps. 143:7)

But along with David's anguish we see his faith.

You can be sure of this: The Lord set apart the godly for himself. The Lord will answer when I call to him. (Ps. 4:3)

But let all who take refuge in you rejoice; let them sing joyful praises forever. Spread your protection over them, that all who love your name may be filled with joy. For you bless the godly, O Lord; you surround them with your shield of love. (Ps. 5:11-12)

Let me hear of your unfailing love each morning, for I am trusting you. Show me where to walk, for I give myself to you. Rescue me from my enemies, Lord; I run to you to hide me. Teach me to do your will, for you are my God. May your gracious Spirit lead me forward on a firm footing. (Ps. 143:8-10)

Amen, Father. Amen.

1. Beth Moore, *Believing God* (Nashville: LifeWay, 2004), 64.
2. Richard Foster, *Prayer: Finding the Heart's True Home* (New York: Harper Collins, 1992), 47-56.

Parenting in Grief

I will always be grateful that our children were young adults when our lives were shattered. Both lived in other cities and had active lives of their own. That's not to say that our forced resignation did not impact them, because it impacted them greatly. But parenting adult children is vastly different from parenting children who are still living at home.

Recently I visited with Julie, a young woman whose husband, Jim, served for five years as youth minister at a local church before being terminated. "Budget cuts" was the reason given publicly by the personnel committee but everyone knew other issues were involved. For months parishioners had watched as the staff turnover rate skyrocketed. Some even joked that they anxiously read the church bulletin each Sunday morning to see who was still listed as "Church Staff."

But Julie and Jim didn't joke. They have young children and their lives have been turned upside down. Every member of the family grieves for what they've lost.

Parenting through times of grief presents a daunting responsibility. Your life has been shattered by the events surrounding your forced resignation and grief shrouds your very existence. You grieve the loss of your job, your ministry, your reputation. And in the midst of your own grief you see the pain and confusion that envelopes your children's lives. They see you cry frequently but don't know why. They sense your stress but don't understand what's happening. All they know is that they don't get to go back to their church and, in many cases, they've lost their friends. As a parent, your natural tendency is to protect your children from grief. But you can't. As renowned grief educator Dr. Earl Grollman has said, "The only cure for grief is to grieve."

I do not pretend to know how to help children cope with great loss, but there are many experts who have knowledge and wisdom to guide you through this time if you have children living at home. One excellent book is *Parenting Through Crisis: Helping Kids in Times of Loss, Grief, and Change* by Barbara Coloroso.[1] Based on her expertise, let's consider what you can do to help your children as they grieve their loss.

Infants—That's right. Even an infant knows when something is wrong. They can sense the change in the emotional climate of the home. They may become irritable and their eating and sleeping habits may change. What they need from you or a trusted friend or grandparent is a loving, gentle touch. Soft talking and singing can provide great comfort.

Toddlers—Toddlers may not understand the cause of your sadness but they can read your mood and they know something is wrong. They may revert back to behaviors such as clinging or sucking their thumb. Any parent would agree it's frustrating to work hard to help your children overcome a negative behavior, only to see them wind up right back where they started as a result of sadness and uncertainty.

Toddlers need the same gentle responses that an infant needs: loving, gentle touches and soothing words. But while toddlers need the same gentle responses that infants need, they do understand basic conversation, so experts suggest that you talk with them about why you are sad and then explain what you are going to do in the immediate future. Including toddlers in future events, like planning a visit to Grandma's house, lets them know that life goes on. And doing something immediate, like watching their favorite afternoon cartoon, provides a sense of routine. Toddlers need this consistency. By taking care of their physical needs and keeping their routines on schedule, you're reassuring them that they are safe and that their needs will be met.

Preschoolers—Preschoolers understand language much better than they can use it. This means that they simply do not have the ability to put their emotions into words. Give them loving attention and keep their routines as normal as possible. And be prepared to answer their questions. They may even ask the same question repeatedly.

"Oh my, this describes our 5-year-old to a T," Julie sighed. "It's been months since Jim was let go and she continues to say, 'Mommy, why can't we go back to our old church?'"

Repeatedly asking the same question is not meant to annoy parents. It simply means children are trying to process information and processing takes time. So patiently answer their questions, reassuring them that you are there for them.

5- to 9-year-olds—Children who are 5 to 9 years old may fluctuate between needing affection and shunning affection altogether, so don't be surprised if your child rejects your reassuring hug. Determining the right time to give affection can be a challenge. Nevertheless, encourage your child to grieve openly at home or with a trusted friend. Let them know of your willingness to listen and prepare them for what they might experience as they grieve. Otherwise, they will be caught off guard when strange emotions erupt and they have no idea how to identify them, much less know what to do with them. Assure your child that their emotions are OK and encourage them to talk to you about what they're feeling.

In his book *A Grace Disguised*, author Jerry Sittser tells about a time following the death of his wife, mother and 4-year-old daughter when his 7-year-old son climbed into his lap late one night, wanting to talk. His young son sat quietly in his lap for a moment before his grief began pouring out. Sittser describes his son's expression of grief as "rage" against the drunk driver who had caused his family so much pain. The little boy who had lost his mother, grandmother and sister wanted the drunk driver to hurt as much as he did. More precisely, Sittser's son wanted to be the one to cause the man's pain.[2]

What strikes me about this story is that Sittser's 7-year-old son felt the freedom to grieve openly with his dad. He knew that he could express his feelings without fear of being reprimanded or punished for them.

Preteens—Bless their hearts, preteens live trapped in a world between childhood and adolescence. They may be reluctant to express their grief through tears for fear of being called a baby. They may pretend that your forced resignation does not affect them at all, when in reality all they want to know is how the resignation is going to impact their everyday life. Outwardly, they may complain of physical ailments such as headaches and stomachaches. Preteens need the same affection and reassurance as younger children. Encourage them to openly share their emotions with you and assure them that their pain will eventually subside.

> **All they want to know is how the resignation is going to impact their everyday life.**

Adolescents—If you are in the process of parenting an adolescent, or if you have survived that time of life, then you know that one word describes adolescents: unpredictable. They love on you like a puppy one moment and bring out the cat claws the next. By nature, they will argue just for the sake of arguing. They live at the center of their universe and seem committed to honing their critical thinking skills by challenging every statement you make.

When you add to this the changes that your forced resignation has brought about in their lives, you're in for a bumpy ride through grief. Nevertheless, encourage your adolescents to openly share their feelings. But first make it clear that they can cry and verbalize their feelings but they cannot physically hurt themselves or someone else. And then—and this is the hard part—let them say what's on their mind, even though it may increase your own pain. They may express anger at you for having to move, change schools and make new friends. They may very well blame you for their pain.

One teenager had an extremely difficult time handling his dad's forced resignation. "The day the news got out that we'd been terminated, Facebook exploded with posts about what had happened," his mom said. "The problem is, nobody really knows the truth but that hasn't stopped people from posting rumors and outright lies. It's gotten really ugly."

My heart breaks for every adolescent whose parent has been terminated. Being a minister's child is difficult in the best of circumstances, but to experience the grief of forced termination surely presents some of life's toughest challenges. These adolescents must process an awful lot of ugliness. They may not know every specific detail about your termination, but they've heard enough and seen enough to understand what's going on. And no matter how hard you may try to hide the depths of your own grief, they see your pain. They must watch you and their siblings grieve but are helpless to do anything about it. And all the while, they wonder what's in store for their future as a shroud of uncertainty envelopes their life.

Experts say that when you talk to your adolescents about their grief, use open-ended questions to get the conversation going and then listen. Listen a lot. When they ask questions, answer as completely as you can. They may not be willing to share their thoughts and feelings with you and may prefer to open up to a close friend. If that's the case, assure them that you are there for them if they ever decide they want to talk.

Regardless of the age of your children, they need three things from you as they move through the elements of grief. They need your time, your love and your encouragement. While they need these three things throughout their lives, they need them in greater degrees during times of grief.

Children of all ages need to spend time with their parents doing the things that the family has always done together. If your family enjoys watching movies or riding bikes or playing games, continue doing those things. Children need to know that not everything in life has changed.

It goes without saying that children need your love as they grieve. They need extra hugs, kisses and gentle touches. They need to hear the words "I love you," regardless of their age. You may have to get creative with adolescents and demonstrate your love with greeting cards on their nightstands, sticky-note messages on their bathroom mirror and small gifts hidden in their backpacks. Regardless of how independent they may try to appear, they still need to be reminded of your love.

Children also need to be reminded that you believe in them. Your words of encouragement are more important than ever when they grieve, so tell them often that you are proud of them. Praise them when they exhibit a positive attitude. Tell them how grateful you are that you get to be their parent.

One of the most important things to tell your children is that you as a family will get through this painful experience *together*. Yes, each family member has his or her own personal journey of grief to make, but you're in this thing called life *together* and *together*, with God's help, you will get through it. They need to hear this message from you and they need to hear it often. It's your statement of faith. You might be saying it through your tears, but the words need to be said, for your sake and for theirs.

You're in this thing called life together and together, with God's help, you will get through it.

Experts agree that parents should answer their children's questions openly and honestly as a child deals with grief. But this presents a huge problem for ministry families. How much can you tell your children about what happened "down at the church"? You can tell them some details, but you cannot tell them everything they may want to know. Facts that are known through a counseling session with a church member cannot be shared with anyone, let alone your children. Sharing confidential information is unethical. And even when the information is known to a large number of church members, it would be inappropriate to share much of it with children. So answering children's questions about why you no longer take them to their church activities and why you're packing boxes to move (even though you may have no idea where you'll be moving to) is a tough job. Your children may want answers to their questions (*What did Deacon Jones say in the meeting?*), but if you cannot divulge the information, explain that the information is confidential and that you're not allowed to share it. Without realizing it, your children will learn the meaning of integrity.

The older I've grown, the more comfortable I've become with admitting that I don't know the answers to life's tough questions. Shortly after we were forced to resign, I ran into a man from the church who said, "I just don't understand what happened." I simply replied, "We don't understand either." If you don't know the answer to their question (*Why is God allowing this to happen?*), admit that you don't know. Children need to learn that God is bigger than our finite minds can comprehend.

Admitting that you don't know the answers to a lot of questions, while affirming your belief that God will take care of you and provide for your needs, demonstrates what it means to walk by faith.

There is no simple way to parent through grief.

There is no simple way to parent through grief. For some, the temptation will be to turn every moment into a "teachable" moment. And certainly there will be many moments that can be used as "teachable" moments. But imagine what would have happened if, when Jerry Sittser's son declared that he wanted to hurt the drunk driver, Sittser had told his son that Jesus wants us to love our enemies. Would that have helped the little boy's grief? Would he have opened up to his dad the next time his grief was too much to bear?

The challenge for couples who have been forced to resign is to allow their children to grieve, to hold them when they cry out in pain, and to find moments to encourage them spiritually without preaching at them. And, to make the challenge even greater, parenting through grief occurs when you are grieving, too. Assure your children, whatever age they may be, that it's OK for them to grieve. It's OK to let your children see you cry, and it's OK for them to know you are seeking answers. Remind them frequently, and remind yourself, that together you will eventually make it through this time of pain.

1. Barbara Coloroso, *Parenting Through Crisis: Helping Kids in Times of Loss, Grief, and Change* (New York: Harper Collins, 2000).

2. Jerry Sittser, *A Grace Disguised: How the Soul Grows Through Loss*, Expanded Edition (Grand Rapids: Zondervan, 2004), 75.

The Power of Response

Much of life is beyond our control. We can enjoy health one day and face surgery the next. The economy can be strong when the market opens and fragile by the time it closes. We can be exceptional behind the wheel yet have a texting driver run a red light and total our car. Church members can love us one Sunday and demand our resignation the next.

We simply cannot control many things in life. Nor can we change what has already happened. But what has happened is only part of the equation. The most important part is how we respond and we do have control over that. As Maya Angelou once said, "You may not control all the events that happen to you, but you can decide not to be reduced by them."

Response is a choice. It's our choice. While we cannot change what has happened, how we respond to what has happened will change us.

While we cannot change what has happened, how we respond to what has happened will change us.

Responding to God in Suffering

Response is a powerful thing. Consider Job. He lost his property, he lost his children, he lost his health and he lost his friends. Yet he remained faithful to God. He held on to his belief that one day he would see God face to face. Throughout much of his suffering, Job's cries to God went unanswered, but his faith remained intact.

Job's wife grieved differently from her husband. She is famous for the advice she gave Job to "curse God and die." She's been criticized in countless sermons and Bible studies and, indeed, there once was the day when I thought she was a poor excuse for a wife.

But during the months we lived with my father-in-law, I began to see Job's wife from a different perspective. Dare I say, I began to identify with her. It occurred to me that when Job lost his property, his children and his friends, *she lost those things, too.* And, on top of such enormous loss, she had to watch her husband suffer ghastly health problems. So, while I do not approve of her words, I understand the agony from which she spoke them.

The book of Job illustrates the importance of response in our lives. Job repeatedly chose to remain faithful to God, even as his friends blamed him for his suffering. "Surely you must have done something wrong, Job, to bring about such a disaster," they said. They were certain his situation was his own fault.

Though they may not say it to your face, many church members respond to the news of a minister's dismissal much like Job's friends. "Well, he surely did *something.* After all, churches don't fire a minister for no reason! I wonder what he did. Have you heard anything?"

As one minister's wife told me when things began to unravel at their church, "I run into people I considered to be friends and I can tell by the way they act that they wonder what we did. Instead of standing up for us, they're wondering if the gossip they've heard is true."

> **"Instead of standing up for us, they're wondering if the gossip they've heard is true."**
> **–Kim**

If you've been forced to resign unjustly, you can take comfort in the fact that Jesus knows exactly what you're going through. For many ministers, uncanny parallels exist between the events of Jesus' ministry and death and the events of their own ministry and resignation.

From the outset, religious leaders criticized and slandered Jesus. The Pharisees were confident of one thing. They were right and anyone who didn't agree with them was wrong. So it didn't take long for their criticism of Jesus to start. They criticized Jesus' ministry from the outset, appalled He would eat meals with "sinners" and heal broken bodies on the Sabbath. Soon their criticism turned to slander as they accused Jesus of being "empowered by the prince of demons" (Matt. 9:34).

Criticism is one thing but slander is a whole different beast. Criticism typically attacks your actions while slander attacks who you are as a person. Criticism, when offered with right motives and in the right manner (something the Pharisees never managed), can be valuable and lead to growth. Slander, by definition, maliciously destroys relationships and reputations. No good ever comes of it.

Early in Jesus' ministry, the Pharisees began plotting His death. Criticizing Jesus didn't satisfy the Pharisees because clearly He wasn't going away. Everywhere He went, crowds followed. So the religious leaders took their hatred a step further. Instead of just criticizing, they began plotting Jesus' assassination. After Jesus healed a man on the Sabbath, "the Pharisees called a meeting to plot how to kill Jesus" (Matt. 12:14).

While those who opposed you probably did not plot your physical death, at least a few made it their personal mission to stop anything you tried to do. They weren't happy until your ministry died and you were gone. As one woman quietly observed, "There's a Judas in every congregation."

> "There's a Judas in every congregation."
> —Beverly

I would add that Pharisees also populate every congregation— leaders who have been in charge for years and they're not going to give up their power just because God led you to take steps with which the leaders (or their wives) disagree. Regardless of what you did, this small but lethal opposition criticized your every move. They undermined your work and, because other church leaders refused to challenge them, they ultimately destroyed your ministry. As Edmund Burke so eloquently stated, "The only thing necessary for the triumph of evil is for good men to do nothing."

Occasionally strong church leaders confront the power hungry critics, but more often than not, the critics remain unchallenged and cause the destruction of godly men and women, leaving ministry families devastated in the wake of their words and actions.

Religious leaders stirred up the crowd. When Jesus stood trial, Pilate didn't find any basis for the charges made against Him by the religious leaders. But the leaders were determined to get rid of Jesus so they "stirred up the crowd" (Mark 15:11).

Tragically, many church leaders follow the example of the Pharisees and "stir up" the congregation. Phone calls, emails, and hush-hush hallway meetings occur as one group vies for the support of their "side" while shoring up opposition against a minister.

After taking a group of young adults on a mission trip to Haiti, one minister, Jake, returned home to face what he describes as "the inquisition." First, Jake was called before the Personnel Committee to answer charges of poor job performance. "I asked them to give me some specific examples but they couldn't name a single thing," he said. "And when I asked to know the names of my accusers, I was told that their identities were confidential."

After the Personnel Committee came the Board of Elders. "They claimed they were upset about my interpretation of the book of Revelation," Jake said, "which was really strange because it had been a couple of years since I'd preached on Revelation. And I'd received no negative feedback after those sermons. So clearly something else was going on, I just didn't know what it was. The only thing that was clear is that they wanted me gone. They'd made up their minds long before they talked with me."

In the weeks following his termination, Jake struggled to make sense of what had happened. What he discovered was that a small handful of church leaders were bothered by Jake's passion for overseas missions (*We shouldn't be spending so much money over there when we have needs right in our own back yard!*). "Oh, let's be honest," Jake said. "It was all about money. These men wanted the church to have a nice fat nest egg, and I saw money as something to use to spread the Gospel."

But instead of taking the issue to Jake with the desire to find a solution, those who disagreed with Jake's passion for ministering overseas "stirred up" the Personnel Committee and the Elders with the goal to get Jake fired. A half-truth here. A speculation there. Stir, stir, stir. "By the time I returned from Haiti, minds were made up. I never stood a chance."

Jesus' accusers twisted His words, taking them out of context and using them against Him. "We heard him say, 'I will destroy this Temple made with human hands, and in three days I will build another, made without human hands'" (Mark 14:58). "This man has been leading our people astray by telling them not to pay their taxes to the Roman government and by claiming he is the Messiah, a king" (Luke 23:2). Jesus' accusers were masters at manipulating language for their own benefit.

Unfortunately, ministers' words are twisted and taken out of context far too often. And when someone is determined to destroy a minister, his own words provide a quick and easy weapon, as one minister discovered.

"I've always felt it was my responsibility as a pastor to stay on top of what's going on in our denomination," Andy began. "Unfortunately, our denomination is in serious trouble. I'd heard rumblings about a split so I started attending meetings held by people on both sides of the conflict. I was just trying to get the facts firsthand. That's all."

After returning from one of the meetings, Andy shared what he'd learned with some of the elders. "My goal was simply to share the facts. But before long, one of the elders twisted my words, took them completely out of context, and suddenly I was portrayed as wanting to lead our church away from the mainstream group. People even thought I was in favor of a denominational split," Andy said.

Andy's goal had been to help his parishioners understand what was happening in their denomination. "But all it took was one person twisting my words, misrepresenting my intentions. In no time, this elder singlehandedly undermined my role as pastor. No matter how hard I tried, I couldn't untangle the twisted words."

Within just a few months, it became clear that Andy would have to leave. "My beliefs had not changed. My love for the parishioners had not changed. But once my words were taken out of context and used against me, there was no way to undo the damage that had been done."

People who had cheered Christ at His triumphal entry into Jerusalem soon changed their tune and called for his death. When Jesus entered Jerusalem, the crowds cheered their King, waving palm branches and shouting "Hosanna!" But in only a matter of days, "Hosanna!" turned to "Crucify Him!" Jesus knew their hearts so the change of cheers to jeers did not take Him by surprise.

The same cannot always be said of clergy couples. The realization that the same people who used to hug your neck now stab you in the back is shocking. Watching people turn and walk away when they see you approaching is baffling. These same people bunked with you on mission trips. You worked with them in VBS. You sang with them in choir. You sat with them at the hospital while a loved one had surgery. You held them when they cried and stood beside them in their darkest hours. They often told you how much you meant to them. How could their hearts have changed so drastically?

When Jesus needed them most, His friends deserted him. One of the saddest verses in the Bible is Matthew 26:56. Armed soldiers had just arrested Jesus and "At that point, all the disciples deserted him and fled."

Every minister who has ever been forced to resign understands the loneliness of that verse. At a time when you needed people to stand and voice their support of you, they deserted you and disappeared. When you were forced to "stand trial" before a group of deacons and elders, you stood alone because everyone else had either fled or joined your accusers.

When we lose our church, our home, our friends and our reputation, the only thing we can control is our response. How should we respond to slander? According to Jesus' teaching, we should remember that we're in good company and consider ourselves blessed:

[11]God blesses you when people mock you and persecute you and lie about you and say all sorts of evil things against you because you are my followers. [12]Be happy about it! Be very glad! For a great reward awaits you in heaven. And remember, the ancient prophets were persecuted in the same way. (Matt. 5:11-12)

The apostle Paul responded to slander this way:

[12]When we are cursed, we bless; when we are persecuted, we endure it; [13]when we are slandered, we answer kindly. (1 Cor. 4:12b-13a NIV)

And the apostle Peter encouraged the dispersed Christians to respond with gentleness and respect:

[14]But even if you should suffer for what is right, you are blessed. "Do not fear their threats; do not be frightened." [15]But in your hearts revere Christ as Lord. Always be prepared to give an answer to everyone who asks you to give the reason for the hope that you have. But do this with gentleness and respect, [16]keeping a clear conscience, so that those who speak maliciously against

*your good behavior in Christ may be ashamed of their slander. (1
Pet. 3:14-16 NIV)*

While the Bible has a lot to say about responding to slander, it
has far less to say (directly, at least) about how to respond in other
situations that arise. How should we respond as our ministries
unravel and we are forced to deal with the aftermath?

When we look at how Jesus responded to those who undermined His ministry, turned people against Him and ultimately
killed Him, we see Someone who kept His focus. Unlike many
ministers who are surprised to discover the identity of their enemies and the maliciousness of their actions, Jesus knew what the
Pharisees were up to all along. He recognized their plots and their
schemes, but He did not allow their schemes to dictate His actions.
Jesus faithfully obeyed God the Father and carried out God's plan.
Shortly before His death, Jesus prayed, "I brought glory to you
here on earth by completing the work you gave me to do" (John
17:4). Jesus determined in His heart to bring glory to the Father,
regardless of how it impacted His own life.

*Father God, I will be responding to the consequences of termi-
nation for the rest of my life. May my thoughts and actions
not be dictated by the behavior of others, but may I seek to
always live so that my life brings glory to your name.*

Responding to God while Moving On

With each step of our journey of grief, my husband and I have
tried to obey God. But obeying God means knowing what He
wants you to do and, as mentioned in the chapter on acceptance,
God sometimes remained quiet for extended periods of time. For
months, He didn't reveal what lay ahead for us.

For many ministers, darkness often accompanies such times of
Divine quietness—a type of blindness that occurs when you have
no idea what God plans to do. You continue to put one foot in front

of the other, but you cannot see where you're going. You simply trust God to keep you from falling.

Jesus had a lot of experience dealing with blindness when He ministered on the earth. In Matthew 9:27-30, Jesus healed two blind men by touching and speaking to them. In Mark 8:22-26, He healed a man's blindness when He spat on his eyes. John 9:1-7 tells us about a time when Jesus put mud on a blind man's eyes and told him to go wash. And in Matthew 20:29-34, Jesus healed two blind men by touching their eyes.

These stories hold important truths regarding healthy responses to God as we move through our journey of grief. The first truth lies in the question Jesus posed to the two blind men in Matthew 9:28. "Do you believe I can make you see?" We must believe that God is good and that He can make our lives good again. We must believe that He loves us and that He will ultimately lead us out of the darkness into light. Essentially, we must continue to believe all that we ever knew to be true about God before our grief journey began, for God has not changed even though our lives have drastically changed.

The second truth found in these stories lies in another question. Two blind men sitting on the side of the road heard that Jesus was approaching and began calling out to Him for mercy. When Jesus drew nearer and heard their cries, He stopped and asked, "What do you want me to do for you?" (Matt. 20:32). Why did Jesus ask a question with such an obvious answer? I believe it's because He wanted the men to verbalize their desire. Yes, God knows our need before we ask (Matt. 6:8), but it's important that we put the desires of our heart into words.

God has not changed even though our lives have drastically changed.

The two blind men knew exactly what they wanted. For ministers who have been forced to resign, however, the answer to Jesus' question, "What do you want me to do for you?" might not be as obvious. When your life has been derailed, it takes many hours in prayer to process the past and discern your desires for the future. "What do you want me to do for you?" can be a difficult question to answer.

The third truth found in these stories emerges from Mark's account of Jesus healing a blind man at Bethsaida. In this encounter, healing was not instantaneous. Jesus first spit on the man's eyes and touched them, and when the man opened his eyes he said, "I see people, but I can't see them very clearly. They look like trees walking around" (8:24). I wonder what went through the man's mind at that moment. Had Jesus failed to heal him completely? Was he doomed to live the rest of his life with only partial healing? Jesus had healed other blind people instantaneously. Why not him? Should he walk away and settle for blurred vision? Or was his faith strong enough to trust Jesus for complete healing. But then Jesus put His hands on the man's eyes a second time and restored his vision completely.

Here's the truth in the Bethsaida story: sometimes moving from darkness into the light is a process, not an event. For whatever reason, Jesus chose to heal the blind man at Bethsaida in two stages. He'd healed other blind people with one touch or one word that brought instantaneous healing, but not this time. That often is what happens with ministers who have been forced to resign. Their journey out of darkness unfolds as a series of transitional steps rather than occurring as an instantaneous event. With each step toward light, we're forced to make a choice. Will we give up on Jesus and settle for blurred vision or will we continue to trust Him to work all things for our good?

The fourth story of healing provides another truth: sometimes we must take action in order to move out of the darkness. In John 9, we read of Jesus' encounter with a man who had been blind from birth. Jesus spat on the ground, made mud and applied it to the man's eyes. Then He told the man to wash in the pool of Siloam (9:6-7). The conciseness of Jesus' instructions intrigues

Sometimes moving from darkness into the light is a process, not an event.

me. Jesus simply told the man to wash in the pool of Siloam. He didn't promise that the man would be able to see after he washed. He didn't tell the man to wash and then return for further instructions. Jesus just said to go wash. The man obeyed, not knowing what would happen. He demonstrated his faith by stumbling his way across town to the pool and washing his eyes. His obedience was rewarded with sight.

As we transition from the darkness of pain into the light of a new life, we will hear the voice of the Holy Spirit tell us to "go wash." Our "washing" may involve applying for a job, moving to a new town, attending a meeting, making a phone call or accepting a job. Our "washing" may not make a lot of sense at the time, but bumbling through town with mud smeared across his face probably didn't make a lot of sense to the blind man either. It's only after we obey that we begin to see the light.

When looking closely at all of the accounts of Jesus healing blind men, one additional truth becomes evident: Jesus dealt with each situation in a personal way. He did not have a pat response but instead He used different methods of healing. In Matthew 9 Jesus touched the men's eyes and spoke words of healing. In Matthew 20, He used touch alone to heal. In Mark 8, He spit on the man's eyes, and in John 9 He spit on the ground and made mud for the man's eyes.

Not only did Jesus use different methods of healing, but He chose the method. Mark 8:22 says that when Jesus and His disciples arrived in Bethsaida, "some people brought a blind man to Jesus, and they begged him to touch the man and heal him." These people had faith that Jesus could heal their friend by touching him. Perhaps they'd seen Jesus heal others by touch, or maybe they had heard the testimony of the man who declared, "But I know this: I was blind, and now I can see!" (John 9:25). In any event, they believed that Jesus could heal. And Jesus did heal—just not in the way they had requested. The people had asked Jesus to heal by touch but in this situation, Jesus healed in two stages: by spitting on the man's eyes followed by His touch. Clearly, Jesus was in charge of how He worked in each individual life.

This is a difficult lesson to learn as we move from darkness into light, but our response to God while moving on is vital to our spiritual health. It's easy to look at God working in another minister's life and ask, "But God, why don't you do that for me?" In recent years, I've known ministers who've sold cars and worked in retail stores after being forced to resign their churches. Others have started up their own house churches and some have established nonprofit ministries. And still others, though few in number, have gone on to serve other churches. In every situation, God has worked in whatever way He deemed best. His sovereignty, though at times not understood, can be trusted, for He is a God of mercy and grace.

Father God, as I move through the blinding pain of termination into the light of a new life, may I refrain from comparing my healing to that of others. May I rest in the knowledge that you are my personal, loving Father who cares more for me than I can possibly imagine. Whether you touch or spit or apply mud to my life, I will trust and I will obey.

Epilogue
The Miracle of Healing

When it became clear we would be living with my father-in-law for an indefinite period of time, I began working for an employment agency. We might not have housing expenses but we did have a son in college and we were determined to meet our financial commitments. Besides, I needed to get out of the house. So I completed the required assessments and began taking temp jobs at businesses needing someone to fill in for vacationing employees. Unfortunately, the agency frequently sent me to title companies. Not good. Not good at all. Granted, they had no way of knowing I was living in one room of my father-in-law's house, but working at title companies where I watched happy couples sign the closing documents on their new homes was more than I could handle.

One day I decided it would be better to work part-time at one business rather than float from one business to another as a temp employee, so I answered an ad at a bookstore. When I met the manager he admitted there were no openings; the ad was just a ploy to collect applications in case they needed to hire someone at a later time. I left the store appalled at such a tactic. But since I was dressed for a job interview I decided to continue my quest.

Hours later, weary and disappointed, I summoned my last ounce of courage, put on my best smile and walked into another bookstore. When I asked to speak with the manager, the clerk asked the dreaded question, "May I tell him what this is about?" I knew if I said I was looking for a job she might tell me they weren't hiring, so I replied, "I'm an author and I wanted to drop by and say hello." No, it wasn't the motive behind my visit but it wasn't a lie.

I was an author and the store did sell curriculum that I'd written and a book that I'd co-authored. I just didn't say I was dropping by in hopes of landing a job. So while the clerk went to the back of the store to get the manager, I quickly located the curriculum section and tried to look calm.

A few minutes later the manager found me. He introduced himself as Victor and I introduced myself as one of his authors. We chatted and I explained that my husband and I had moved back to the area and I was looking for part-time work. Victor hired me on the spot and told me to come back the next morning to complete the official application process. As I drove back to the house I felt something deep inside that I hadn't felt in nearly a year. It took me a moment to recognize that for the first time since our forced resignation, I had hope.

The next morning I returned to the store and completed the official job interview in the manager's office. Victor went through his official list of questions and I breezed through each answer effortlessly. But then he asked a question that stopped me cold.

"Where do you see yourself five years from now?" he asked.

Suddenly I couldn't speak. My throat tightened and tears filled my eyes as I struggled to control my emotions. When I finally regained my composure I said, "10 months ago I could have answered that question. But now I have no idea." I then shared the whole story. When I finished, Victor responded by sharing his own story. As it turned out, his father had been a minister and had been forced to resign his church. Victor knew firsthand what forced resignation did to a minister and to the minister's family. He had also been through an ugly divorce. He knew what it meant for life to suddenly shatter. He'd experienced his own betrayal and intense grief.

As I talked with Victor, I knew without any doubt that this job was God's gift to me. On mornings when I was scheduled to open the store, Victor and I spent time reading a devotional and praying for each other. He always asked about my husband and faithfully prayed for him. I, in return, asked about his new wife, his daughter, and the challenges he faced in graduate school. We talked. We prayed. I cried.

And slowly I began to heal.

During the months that followed, scabs began to form over the raw wounds as I allowed myself to receive love and acceptance from my co-workers. Most of them were college students, the same age as my own kids, and I gained strength just being around them. They never knew my story but they welcomed me to the store and patiently taught me how to shelve books, create displays and run the cash register. Hebrews 1:14 refers to ministering angels and, in many ways, Victor and my co-workers were my ministering angels. I will forever be in their debt for putting me on the path to healing.

The healing that began in that bookstore nearly six years ago continues today. I'm not completely healed, but the tender scars far outnumber the raw wounds. Today my husband and I own a beautiful home; we have true friends—people who love and care about us because of who we are, not because of my husband's job title; and we work for extraordinary nonprofit organizations that minister to people in need. On a daily basis, we work with people whose lives have been shattered, people who need jobs, people who need encouragement, people who want a stable place to call home.

I'm not completely healed, but the tender scars far outnumber the raw wounds.

In addition to running a nonprofit, my husband stays in constant demand as an interim pastor. God uses him to strengthen congregations and prepare them for new leadership. Without exception, the members of every church he has served as interim have wanted him to stay as their full-time pastor, but he's never felt God leading him to accept a permanent pastorate. Instead, God continues to expand his sphere of influence as he faithfully preaches the Word to multiple congregations.

Recently, a friend asked me what I've learned on my journey of grief. While many unanswered questions still remain, three lessons have significantly impacted my life. The first lesson is that God really does work all things together for the good of those who love Him: those who are called according to His purpose (Rom. 8:28). I had always known that truth on one level, but these past six years have taught me this truth on a much deeper level. I have experienced firsthand what God can do. I do not for one moment believe God caused our forced resignation, nor do I believe it was His perfect will. But for reasons I do not understand, He allowed our lives to be shattered and He has brought beauty from the brokenness and pain.

Second, I learned to quit expecting to "recover" from the trauma of forced resignation. I had to accept the fact I would never fully "recover" but I could learn a new way to live. For the rest of my life memories will surface that trigger anger or sadness. There will always be days when I shake my head in disbelief when I remember what happened. The effects of how we were treated will always be with me, influencing my relationships with friends, co-workers and congregations. I will always be dealing with the elements of grief to some degree as I move on through life.

The third lesson I have learned while working on this book is that grief and joy can co-exist. It is possible to experience joy and grief simultaneously. It was a difficult lesson to learn, for I had to let go of my desire for life to be the way it was before our forced resignation. I had to

> **It is possible to experience joy and grief simultaneously.**

come to grips with the fact that life would never be that way again. I have changed. My husband has changed. Memories of the church we loved dearly will always bring a twinge of sadness, but just because life is not the way it used to be does not mean we cannot live happy, fulfilling lives serving the Lord today.

Six years into my journey of grief and grace, I can honestly say that life is good. No, life is *very* good. It is not the life my husband and I had planned. It is nothing like the first 30 years of our marriage and ministry. We would never have chosen to travel this road. But God in His infinite mercy and grace has made beauty out of ugliness. He has blessed us beyond what we ever imagined possible. When I consider where we are today, I'm reminded of how the story of Job ends: "So the Lord blessed Job in the second half of his life even more than in the beginning" (Job 42:12).

I actually started to write this book three years into our grief journey but the process was too painful so I set it aside. But then an event happened in December 2013 that revealed it was time to pick up the project again. I was on my way to work and while stopped in traffic I grabbed a random CD, popped it into the player, and pressed play. For the rest of my drive I celebrated the holidays as I enjoyed beautiful piano music. It wasn't until I pulled into the parking lot at my office that I realized I'd been listening to the CD of Christmas carols with piano and handbells that had once caused such pain. Only now, the music brought joy rather than sorrow. Somewhere along the way, my heart had begun to heal. One day, yours will too.

Appendix

An Open Letter to Churches

Resources for Surviving the Grief of Forced Termination

An Open Letter to Churches

Dear Church,

On behalf of all the ministers who have not experienced forced resignation, allow me to say a few words that they may not feel free to express themselves.

Let's start by talking numbers. Every church, regardless of denomination, keeps track of numbers. They keep track of how many people participate in Bible study, worship services, Vacation Bible School, revival services, mission trips, retreats, conferences, committee meetings, children's activities, youth events and choir rehearsals. And then there are the numbers preceded by dollar signs. Periodically, churches hold meetings to discuss the receipt and disbursement of every dollar. There's no question that numbers represent vital information in the life of a church. Unfortunately, many lay people equate numbers with success. The higher the number, the greater the success. But that's not always the case. Plenty of churches have lots of people and plenty of money and busy calendars, but the Holy Spirit is nowhere to be found.

But that's a discussion for another time.

For now, Church, I want to share with you a specific number— one that perhaps you've never considered:

80% of ministers believe pastoral ministry has had a negative impact on their families[1]

Eighty percent!

I'm not surprised. Just appalled. You should be appalled, too.

Many people don't understand why ministry has a negative impact on ministers' families but there are many reasons for this negativity. I want to touch on three of them.

One reason pastoral ministry negatively impacts a minister's family is the amount of scrutiny they must endure. Shortly after becoming a pastor's wife, I lay on the sofa while recovering from the flu and watched the television coverage of the first inauguration of Ronald Reagan. Much of the attention focused, of course, on the new president. But an inordinate amount of attention—and camera time—focused on the president's wife. Television reporters analyzed Nancy Reagan from top to bottom. Literally. Everything from her hat, her hair, her earrings, her smile, her dress, her coat, her gloves and her shoes—everything received a detailed analysis. I remember thinking, "Wow, I never realized I have so much in common with the First Lady."

At the time, we were serving a small church with a couple of difficult deacons' wives. One Sunday, one of them tilted her nose up just a bit and said to me, "Ohhhh, *another* new outfit I see." What she didn't know was that I couldn't remember the last time I'd had a new outfit. My entire wardrobe came from my mother who passed her clothes on to me. Just about everything I possessed had several years' wear on it before finding its way to my closet. I guess I could have explained the source of my clothes to this deacon's wife, but, as it turned out, my attire was just one of the many topics she chose to criticize.

Ministers and their families live with an unreasonable amount of scrutiny. For some reason, many within the body of Christ feel the freedom to criticize those God has led to serve your congregation. I overheard a deacon's wife one Sunday as she criticized the minister's wife for being too outgoing. She openly declared that the young woman should not scurry around the church talking to everyone but should act more reserved (insert "tsk, tsk" here). I can't help but think that had the minister's wife been more reserved, the deacon's wife would have deemed her unfriendly. Pleasing her bordered on the impossible.

Unfortunately, ministers' wives are not the only target of your criticism. Our children make easy targets as well. "Shame on you! You shouldn't say that – wear that – do that – feel that – watch that – read that. Your father is the minister!"

One woman once approached my daughter who was a teenager at the time and criticized her for going to another church with a friend after first attending our church. Seriously? This woman criticized my daughter for going to church too much? She never would have criticized another teenager in the church for going to extra services, yet she felt free to confront my child. Unfortunately, this woman represents a host of others.

Many within the Church will say things to the minister's children that they never would say to any other child. This simply is unfair. One minister's teenage daughter describes the deacons' wives as her "13 menopausal mothers." Living under constant scrutiny weighs her down and makes her life miserable. It's no wonder she never laughs or smiles.

Dear Church, when you stop and consider the critical scrutiny lavished upon ministers' families, you can understand why the vast majority of ministers say their families suffer because of pastoral ministry. It's hard enough to live in today's society without constant criticism. Ministers' families are not perfect. They make mistakes, just as every family within the body of Christ makes mistakes. They do not need criticism from you. They need unconditional love, prayers and grace. Come to think of it, these are the same things you need from them.

What can you do to help? Refuse to criticize. Offer words of encouragement and pray for your minister's family. And please, refrain from using terms like "PK," "the preacher's son" or "the youth pastor's daughter." This only sets them apart as being different and they want nothing more than to blend in with the rest of their peers at church. The same thing applies to the minister's wife.

She has a name. She has a life apart from her husband so please get to know her as an individual. You'll probably be pleasantly surprised at the special gifts God has given her.

While we're on the topic of criticism, here's one more thing you can do to help. If you have an issue with your minister, first pray about it. Ask God to show you if the issue is valid. After spending time in prayer, if you're still bothered then go to your minister directly. That's the biblical standard. It's unfair and unbiblical—*it's outright sin*—to go to other people with your grievance before you've even given the minister a chance to resolve the issue.

> **It's outright sin to go to other people with your grievance before you've even given the minister a chance to resolve the issue.**

A second reason pastoral ministry negatively impacts ministers' families is the minister's unreasonable workload. According to a recent study, many ministers work between 55 and 75 hours per week and are on call 24/7.[2] That means when they get home, they're exhausted. It means they often have weeks when they aren't home for supper because they have meetings at the church every night. It means when they do get home they're often on the phone, talking or texting with church members who believe it's their right to communicate with their minister any time of the day or night. It means their children grow up learning that Church has stolen their dad.

I realize that many other professions require heavy workloads too. But here's the difference. Ministers carry the profound awareness that their effectiveness or lack thereof impacts the eternity of those in their care. That's a huge burden to bear.

What can you do to help? For starters, and I don't mean this to sound harsh, but please do not treat your minister as your employee. I truly believe this attitude plays a role in the negative impact on a minister's family. Unlike the secular world where one employer has many employees, in churches there are many employers (the members) and few employees (the ministers). Ministers do not have one boss to please. They must please every member of the congregation. This used to be a bit more bearable because church members respected their ministerial staff, regarding them as people called of God to guide their congregation. Today, however, many church members regard their ministers as hired help. Just as they expect the server at the restaurant to take care of their needs with prompt service, many members expect their minister to take care of their needs, perceived or real, at any time of the day or night. This attitude makes it impossible for the minister to have healthy family relationships. They can't plan family outings, and vacations frequently get cut short (or don't happen at all) when a crisis arises or a church member dies.

So what can you do? Respect your minister's home life. Don't call or drop by during evening hours unless you've been invited to do so. Except for true emergencies, save your calls and visits for office hours. Even Jesus had to get away from the crowds and spend time alone or with His closest friends. If Jesus needed that time to rejuvenate, surely your minister does as well.

Another thing you can do to alleviate the problem of an unreasonable workload is to evaluate the church schedule. Does the minister really need to attend every single meeting and event? Probably not. What many church members don't realize is that when the minister attends a church-wide picnic, they're at a picnic but he is at work. When members insist the minister attend their class social, they're at a party but he is at work. And if he attends one social then he has to attend all socials or else endure the criticism when he's accused of playing favorites. Dear Church, please recognize the impossible demands that you're making on your minister and make necessary adjustments.

A third reason pastoral ministry negatively impacts ministers' families is the number of unrealistic expectations. George Barna once said that "Most pastors work long hours, are constantly on-call, often sacrifice time with family to tend to congregational crises, carry long-term debt from the cost of seminary and receive below-average compensation in return for performing a difficult job. Trained in theology, they are expected to master leadership, politics, finance, management, psychology and conflict resolution."[3]

Seriously, no one can live up to such unrealistic expectations. Add to this the unrealistic expectations put on the minister's family and you begin to understand why pastoral ministry has such a negative impact.

Unrealistic expectations often prevent a minister's wife from being herself. She's constantly on guard, afraid she'll say or do something that meets with your disapproval. And since the majority of her life is spent around church members, she often feels unable to be herself. Before long, many wives lose their identities, fading behind their role as the minister's wife and losing sight of who they really are. But it doesn't have to be this way. Your minister's wife has goals and dreams of her own, apart from her husband. Encourage her to pursue whatever God calls her to do, even if that means she doesn't play the piano, sing in the choir, teach a Bible class or lead the women's mission group. Allow her to be the individual that God has created her to be rather than insisting that she fill a role for which she has no interest or skill.

Many wives lose their identities, fading behind their role as the minister's wife and losing sight of who they really are.

Then, of course, there are the unrealistic expectations put upon ministers' children. Regardless of their age, ministers' children know that their words and actions can cause trouble for their parents. That knowledge does not always keep them from speaking the words or carrying out the action that brings about trouble, but they live with the weight of unrealistic expectations nonetheless.

What can you do to help? Before you expect your minister's wife or children to do something, ask yourself, "Would I expect another woman or child to do this or do I expect it simply because they are part of the minister's family?" The same standards should apply to the minister's family as apply to any other Christian family. But to expect them to be at church every time the door is open and to behave in a way that is beyond their years or experience is to weigh them down with unrealistic expectations and the knowledge that, sooner or later, they will fail you. And they know when they fail to live up to your expectations, you will criticize them. That's just not fair.

Here's another number you should know. It's from a recent Barna Group report.

40% of ministers say their child, age 15 or older, struggled with their faith at some point[4]

Some people may be surprised at this statistic. (These are the same people who think the minister's house never gets dirty, laundry remains clean and pressed, meals meet strict nutritional guidelines, the checkbook balances on the first try, each child makes the honor roll, all conversation centers around Jesus, and each family member speaks gently to one another in King James English.) But the reality is this: ministers' kids are really no different than other kids. They face the same questions, the same temptations and the same struggles. Growing up in a minister's home does not make them immune to life's challenges.

While some people assume that ministers' children will meet life's challenges head-on and ultimately follow in their parents' footsteps and become ministers themselves, or at the very least become active leaders within a church, that's not always the case. Indeed, some do. But others shudder at the thought. In fact, 33% of ministers' children over the age of 15 are no longer even active in a church and 7% have walked away from their faith altogether.[5] What tragic statistics.

What causes ministers' children to struggle with their faith? Barna asked pastors that same question and the number one reason given was unrealistic expectations. I'm not surprised. All children, regardless of their parents' jobs, face enormous stress to succeed in school. Ministers' children, however, have the added stress of unrealistic expectations at church. They're expected to know their Bible backwards and forwards, participate in choir even if they're tone deaf, attend every youth activity and go on every mission trip. And all the while they're expected to be Mr. and Miss Congeniality. Forget that their bodies are growing and developing just like every other kid. Forget that when they hit puberty they're self-conscious about the changes they experience, the blemishes that erupt and the unpredictable minefield known as friendships. Ministers' kids are expected to put all of that aside and demonstrate perfect etiquette in any and all situations.

With such unrealistic expectations, it's a wonder every minister's kid doesn't crash and burn. And when you heap the added chaos of watching your parents struggle and grieve because the church has swept them out with the trash, I'm amazed they don't struggle with their faith even more. When I asked one minister how his son was doing in the aftermath of his forced resignation he hesitated a moment before saying, "Let's just say his commitment isn't what it should be. Churches don't consider the ramifications of forcing a minister to resign." So Church, before you force your minister to resign, please think through all of the ramifications of your actions because they will be felt by many people for many years to come.

Dear Church, here's one final number you should know. When Barna asked these same pastors about parenting regrets,

42% of ministers said they wish they had spent more time with their children[6]

Do you see it, Church? Do you see the vicious cycle that entraps clergy families? Faced with unbearable scrutiny, they accept unreasonable workloads and attempt to meet unrealistic expectations in an effort to curtail your criticism. Many ministers sacrifice their children and marriage relationships upon the altar of church work, mistakenly believing that if they just work longer and harder they will encounter less criticism.

What can you do to help? Insist—no, *demand*—that your ministers take a day off every week and that they take all of the vacation time allotted to them. Allow them uninterrupted time to spend with their families and then respect that time. Refuse to call them "just for a minute" or "with just one question." To put it bluntly, leave them alone when they're with their families.

And by all means, stop expecting them to walk on water. They can't do it—although many ministry families have drowned while trying.

Sincerely yours,
Deanna Harrison

1. Pastoral Care, http://www.pastoralcareinc.com/statistics.
2. Ibid.
3. The Barna Group, "A Profile of Protestant Pastors in Anticipation of 'Pastor Appreciation Month.'" September 25, 2001. www.barna.org.
4. The Barna Group, "Prodigal Pastor Kids: Fact or Fiction?" November 12, 2013. www.barna.org.
5. Ibid.
6. Ibid.

Resources for Surviving
the Grief of Forced Termination

CITY OF REFUGE, a ministry of First Baptist Church, Woodstock, GA
11905 Highway 92
Woodstock, GA 30188
(770) 926-4428
http://www.fbcw.org/
The goal of City of Refuge is "to provide critical care for wounded and fallen ministers, giving them a safe and loving environment in which to grow and heal."

HEALINGCHOICE
5717 66th Street
Lubbock TX 79424
(888) 540-8779
www.healingchoice.org
HealingChoice is a non-profit organization that offers several types of care including help for clergy and clergy families. "If you are serving in ministry or are the family member of a minister, our professional PastorCare counselors may be able to help. We know that ministry can be very demanding and personal or family issues can be difficult to deal with. Our counselors are licensed and experienced with the unique challenges of ministry work."

MARBLE RETREAT

Retreat Address: 181 Bannockburn, Marble, CO 81623
Business Office: P.O. Box 176, Carbondale, CO 81623
(970) 963-2499
Email: MinistryCare@MarbleRetreat.org
www.marbleretreat.org
Marble Retreat is an interdenominational Christian counseling center that provides an opportunity for healing for clergy and others in Christian service. Their mission is "to help bring healing, hope and restoration to those in vocational Christian ministry and the Church at large through Christ-centered brief intensive counseling."

DR. DAN MCGEE, President & CEO

Dan McGee Associates
301 S. Center, Suite 214
Arlington, TX 76010
(817) 276-6412
www.drdanmcgee.com
Along with his sister, Dan McGee co-authored *Beyond Termination: A Spouse's Story of Pain and Healing* in 1990. The book was written after his sister's husband was forced to resign his church. To my knowledge, it is the only other book written specifically for clergy couples on the subject of forced termination of ministers.

SONSCAPE RETREATS

PO Box 700
Divide, CO 80814
(888) 766-7227
Email: info@sonscape.org
www.sonscaperetreats.org/
Sonscape Retreats offers weeklong, guided retreats for clergy who seek "to balance the demands of life, family, and ministry while rekindling their passion for Christ and His church."

SUGGESTED READING

A Grace Disguised: How the Soul Grows Through Loss, by Jerry Sittser, Expanded Edition 2004.

Anger: Handling a Powerful Emotion in a Healthy Way, by Gary Chapman, 2007.

Forgive and Forget: Healing the Hurts We Don't Deserve by Lewis B. Smedes, 1984.

Free Yourself to Love: The Liberating Power of Forgiveness by Jackie Kendall, 2009.

Letting Go of Anger: How to Get Your Emotions Under Control by Annie Chapman, 2010.

Silent God by Joseph Bentz, 2007.

When Your World Falls Apart: Seeing Past the Pain of the Present, by David Jeremiah, 2000.

About the Author

Deanna Harrison is a minister's wife and survivor of forced termination. She holds an MA in English and a BA in Journalism. For over 30 years, Deanna has written Bible study curriculum and numerous articles for clergy couples seeking to grow in ministry. She is also the author of the devotional book *My Ducks Are Really Swans* (Broadman Press). Deanna and her husband, Scott, have two grown children.

To contact the author, visit www.deannaharrison.com.

Photo by Francie Batten Hodges

a Book's Mind

Whether you want to purchase bulk copies of
Moving On
or buy another book for a friend, get it now at:
www.abooksmart.com

If you have a book that you would like to publish,
contact Floyd Orfield, Publisher, at A Book's Mind:
floyd@abooksmind.com.

www.abooksmind.com

CPSIA information can be obtained
at www.ICGtesting.com
Printed in the USA
FSOW03n1336240116
16014FS